WOMEN
IN
AMERICAN INDIAN SOCIETY

WOMEN
IN
AMERICAN INDIAN
SOCIETY

Rayna Green
National Museum of American History
Smithsonian Institution

Frank W. Porter III
General Editor

CHELSEA HOUSE PUBLISHERS
New York   Philadelphia

Frontispiece   A 1903 photograph of Lizzie Cayuse, a prominent Nez Perce woman who accompanied Chief Joseph to the St. Louis Exposition of 1904.

On the cover   *Corn Mother*, an 18″ ceramic sculpture decorated with beads and shells, by Navajo artist Pablita Abeyta, 1989. From the collection of Rayna Green.

Chelsea House Publishers
Editor-in-Chief   Remmel Nunn
Managing Editor   Karyn Gullen Browne
Copy Chief   Mark Rifkin
Picture Editor   Adrian G. Allen
Art Director   Maria Epes
Assistant Art Director   Howard Brotman
Manufacturing Director   Gerald Levine
Systems Manager   Lindsey Ottman
Production Manager   Joseph Romano
Production Coordinator   Marie Claire Cebrián

Indians of North America
Senior Editor   Liz Sonneborn

Staff for **WOMEN IN AMERICAN INDIAN SOCIETY**
Assistant Editor   Leigh Hope Wood
Senior Copy Editor   Laurie Kahn
Editorial Assistant   Michele Berezansky
Designer   Debora Smith
Picture Researcher   Melanie Sanford

5   7   9   8   6   4

Library of Congress Cataloging-in-Publication Data

Green, Rayna.
      Women in American Indian society/by Rayna Green.
          p.   cm.—(Indians of North America)
      Includes bibliographical references and index.
      Summary: Examines the life and culture of North
   American Indian women.
      ISBN 1-55546-734-2
          0-7910-0401-5 (pbk.)
      1. Indians of North America—Women.   2. Indians of
   North America—Social life and customs.   3. Women—North
   America—Social conditions.   [1. Indians of North America—
   Women.   2. Indians of North America—Social life and
   customs.]   I. Title   II. Series: Indians of North America
   (Chelsea House Publishers)
                                                        91-20770
   E98.W8G73   1992   CIP
   305.48′897—dc20   AC

CONTENTS

INDIANS OF NORTH AMERICA

CHELSEA HOUSE PUBLISHERS

INDIANS OF NORTH AMERICA: CONFLICT AND SURVIVAL

Frank W. Porter III

The Indians survived our open intention of wiping them out, and since the tide turned they have even weathered our good intentions toward them, which can be much more deadly.

John Steinbeck
America and Americans

When Europeans first reached the North American continent, they found hundreds of tribes occupying a vast and rich country. The newcomers quickly recognized the wealth of natural resources. They were not, however, so quick or willing to recognize the spiritual, cultural, and intellectual riches of the people they called Indians.

The Indians of North America examines the problems that develop when people with different cultures come together. For American Indians, the consequences of their interaction with non-Indian people have been both productive and tragic. The Europeans believed they had "discovered" a "New World," but their religious bigotry, cultural bias, and materialistic world view kept them from appreciating and understanding the people who lived in it. All too often they attempted to change the way of life of the indigenous people. The Spanish conquistadores wanted the Indians as a source of labor. The Christian missionaries, many of whom were English, viewed them as potential converts. French traders and trappers used the Indians as a means to obtain pelts. As Francis Parkman, the 19th-century historian, stated, "Spanish civilization crushed the Indian; English civilization scorned and neglected him; French civilization embraced and cherished him."

Nearly 500 years later, many people think of American Indians as curious vestiges of a distant past, waging a futile war to survive in a Space Age society. Even today, our understanding of the history and culture of American Indians is too often derived from unsympathetic, culturally biased, and inaccurate reports. The American Indian, described and portrayed in thousands of movies, television programs, books, articles, and government studies, has either been raised to the status of the "noble savage" or disparaged as the "wild Indian" who resisted the westward expansion of the American frontier.

Where in this popular view are the real Indians, the human beings and communities whose ancestors can be traced back to ice-age hunters? Where are the creative and indomitable people whose sophisticated technologies used the natural resources to ensure their survival, whose military skill might even have prevented European settlement of North America if not for devastating epidemics and disruption of the ecology? Where are the men and women who are today diligently struggling to assert their legal rights and express once again the value of their heritage?

The various Indian tribes of North America, like people everywhere, have a history that includes population expansion, adaptation to a range of regional environments, trade across wide networks, internal strife, and warfare. This was the reality. Europeans justified their conquests, however, by creating a mythical image of the New World and its native people. In this myth, the New World was a virgin land, waiting for the Europeans. The arrival of Christopher Columbus ended a timeless primitiveness for the original inhabitants.

Also part of this myth was the debate over the origins of the American Indians. Fantastic and diverse answers were proposed by the early explorers, missionairies, and settlers. Some thought that the Indians were descended from the Ten Lost Tribes of Israel, others that they were descended from inhabitants of the lost continent of Atlantis. One writer suggested that the Indians had reached North America in another Noah's ark.

A later myth, perpetrated by many historians, focused on the relentless persecution during the past five centuries until only a scattering of these "primitive" people remained to be herded onto reservations. This view fails to chronicle the overt and covert ways in which the Indians successfully coped with the intruders.

All of these myths presented one-sided interpretations that ignored the complexity of European and American events and policies. All left serious questions unanswered. What were the origins of the American Indians? Where did they come from? How and when did they get to the New World? What was their life—their culture—really like?

In the late 1800s, anthropologists and archaeologists in the Smithsonian Institution's newly created Bureau of American Ethnology in Washington,

D.C., began to study scientifically the history and culture of the Indians of North America. They were motivated by an honest belief that the Indians were on the verge of extinction and that along with them would vanish their languages, religious beliefs, technology, myths, and legends. These men and women went out to visit, study, and record data from as many Indian communities as possible before this information was forever lost.

By this time there was a new myth in the national consciousness. American Indians existed as figures in the American past. They had performed a historical mission. They had challenged white settlers who trekked across the continent. Once conquered, however, they were supposed to accept graciously the way of life of their conquerors.

The reality again was different. American Indians resisted both actively and passively. They refused to lose their unique identity, to be assimilated into white society. Many whites viewed the Indians not only as members of a conquered nation but also as "inferior" and "unequal." The rights of the Indians could be expanded, contracted, or modified as the conquerors saw fit. In every generation, white society asked itself what to do with the American Indians. Their answers have resulted in the twists and turns of federal Indian policy.

There were two general approaches. One way was to raise the Indians to a "higher level" by "civilizing" them. Zealous missionaries considered it their Christian duty to elevate the Indian through conversion and scanty education. The other approach was to ignore the Indians until they disappeared under pressure from the ever-expanding white society. The myth of the "vanishing Indian" gave stronger support to the latter option, helping to justify the taking of the Indians' land.

Prior to the end of the 18th century, there was no national policy on Indians simply because the American nation had not yet come into existence. American Indians similarly did not possess a political or social unity with which to confront the various Europeans. They were not homogeneous. Rather, they were loosely formed bands and tribes, speaking nearly 300 languages and thousands of dialects. The collective identity felt by Indians today is a result of their common experiences of defeat and/or mistreatment at the hands of whites.

During the colonial period, the British crown did not have a coordinated policy toward the Indians of North America. Specific tribes (most notably the Iroquois and the Cherokee) became military and political pawns used by both the crown and the individual colonies. The success of the American Revolution brought no immediate change. When the United States acquired new territory from France and Mexico in the early 19th century, the federal government wanted to open this land to settlement by homesteaders. But the Indian tribes that lived on this land had signed treaties with European governments assuring their title to the land. Now the United States assumed legal responsibility for honoring these treaties.

At first, President Thomas Jefferson believed that the Louisiana Purchase contained sufficient land for both the Indians and the white population. Within a generation, though, it became clear that the Indians would not be allowed to remain. In the 1830s the federal government began to coerce the eastern tribes to sign treaties agreeing to relinquish their ancestral land and move west of the Mississippi River. Whenever these negotiations failed, President Andrew Jackson used the military to remove the Indians. The southeastern tribes, promised food and transportation during their removal to the West, were instead forced to walk the "Trail of Tears." More than 4,000 men, woman, and children died during this forced march. The "removal policy" was successful in opening the land to homesteaders, but it created enormous hardships for the Indians.

By 1871 most of the tribes in the United States had signed treaties ceding most or all of their ancestral land in exchange for reservations and welfare. The treaty terms were intended to bind both parties for all time. But in the General Allotment Act of 1887, the federal government changed its policy again. Now the goal was to make tribal members into individual landowners and farmers, encouraging their absorption into white society. This policy was advantageous to whites who were eager to acquire Indian land, but it proved disastrous for the Indians. One hundred thirty-eight million acres of reservation land were subdivided into tracts of 160, 80, or as little as 40 acres, and allotted tribe members on an individual basis. Land owned in this way was said to have "trust status" and could not be sold. But the surplus land—all Indian land not allotted to individuals—was opened (for sale) to white settlers. Ultimately, more than 90 million acres of land were taken from the Indians by legal and illegal means.

The resulting loss of land was a catastrophe for the Indians. It was necessary to make it illegal for Indians to sell their land to non-Indians. The Indian Reorganization Act of 1934 officially ended the allotment period. Tribes that voted to accept the provisions of this act were reorganized, and an effort was made to purchase land within preexisting reservations to restore an adequate land base.

Ten years later, in 1944, federal Indian policy again shifted. Now the federal government wanted to get out of the "Indian business." In 1953 an act of Congress named specific tribes whose trust status was to be ended "at the earliest possible time." This new law enabled the United States to end unilaterally, whether the Indians wished it or not, the special status that protected the land in Indian tribal reservations. In the 1950s federal Indian policy was to transfer federal responsibility and jurisdiction to state governments, encourage the physical relocation of Indian peoples from reservations to urban areas, and hasten the termination, or extinction, of tribes.

Between 1954 and 1962 Congress passed specific laws authorizing the termination of more than 100 tribal groups. The stated purpose of the termination policy was to ensure the full and complete integration of Indians into American society. However, there is a less benign way to interpret this legislation. Even as termination was being discussed in Congress, 133 separate bills were introduced to permit the transfer of trust land ownership from Indians to non-Indians.

With the Johnson administration in the 1960s the federal government began to reject termination. In the 1970s yet another Indian policy emerged. Known as "self-determination," it favored keeping the protective role of the federal government while increasing tribal participation in, and control of, important areas of local government. In 1983 President Reagan, in a policy statement on Indian affairs, restated the unique "government is government" relationship of the United States with the Indians. However, federal programs since then have moved toward transferring Indian affairs to individual states, which have long desired to gain control of Indian land and resources.

As long as American Indians retain power, land, and resources that are coveted by the states and the federal government, there will continue to be a "clash of cultures," and the issues will be contested in the courts, Congress, the White House, and even in the international human rights community. To give all Americans a greater comprehension of the issues and conflicts involving American Indians today is a major goal of this series. These issues are not easily understood, nor can these conflicts be readily resolved. The study of North American Indian history and culture is a necessary and important step toward that comprehension. All Americans must learn the history of the relations between the Indians and the federal government, recognize the unique legal status of the Indians, and understand the heritage and cultures of the Indians of North America.

Personification of America (ca. 1595), an engraving by Adrien
Collaert II after Martin de Vos. From reports made by explorers de-
scribing the New World, artists embodied the European vision of the
Americas as a rich, exotic land in the image of the Indian Queen.
Here the Queen is shown bare breasted, holding weapons, and riding
an armadillo, an animal indigenous to the Americas.

RETHINKING
THE
INDIAN WOMAN

Soon after European explorers first arrived in the New World, they began to draw pictures and write descriptions of the land and native peoples they encountered. Inspired by such documents, European artists and writers created their own portraits of these places and people, basing their art more on myth and imagination than on the reality observed and recorded by early explorers.

Certain mythic figures soon dominated the images used in drawings and etchings of the New World. Of these, the Indian Queen came to be perhaps the symbol that best evoked for Europeans an exotic world filled with riches. Representative of this bountiful land, the image of the Indian Queen was large and voluptuous. Usually shown holding or surrounded by pineapples and other fruits, she was dark skinned and bare breasted—the latter was considered a symbol of innocence. She wore a crown of upright feathers and a skirt of leaves, later portrayed as leaves of tobacco, a plant native to the Americas and introduced to Europeans by native peoples. Surrounded by warriors, she carried a spear and often placed her foot on the head of an alligator to show her strength and dominance over all things.

Although the Indian Queen remained a symbol of the Americas for nearly 200 years, the image changed through time. She became thinner, and her skin color grew lighter. She lost her native warriors, her spear, and the fruits of the land. Eventually, she donned a tiara of classical origin and the bracelets of Greek goddesses and covered her breast with the type of white robe often associated with ancient Greece and Rome. The new Queen appeared to be related to Minerva or Diana, the Greco-Roman goddesses of liberty and war, representing a more European, non-Indian America. Wearing a combination of European and Indian clothing, the Statue of Liberty and the statue of "Freedom" on top of the U.S. Capitol are in fact reminiscent of this new Queen.

Although Europeans first associated the Americas with the Indian woman, they understood very little about Indian cultures and the importance of the women within these societies. Even today, most Americans have a poor understanding of the historical importance of Indian women, for very little was written prior to the mid-18th century about women as individuals or as members of a group. Non-Indians who documented history were usually male and intensely interested in business transactions, war, and diplomatic relations. Their texts tended to focus on Indian men in their public and formal roles—as chiefs, warriors, medicine men, and diplomats. But Indian women played equally important roles in the determination and survival of their people.

As stated by Ponca leader Standing Bear, his mother, Pretty Face, " . . . in her humble way, helped to make the history of her race. For it is the mothers, not her warriors, who create a people and guide her destiny." Because of the way history has been recorded, Indian war chiefs, such as Geronimo, Sitting Bull, and Red Cloud, have become well-known figures; Indian women of significant historical importance have not.

Historians have shortchanged Indian cultures by not presenting the women in their fairly standard roles as traders, farmers, artisans, and healers.

Furthermore, although historians have failed to portray Indian men as fathers, brothers, and husbands, even less has been written about Indian women in terms of their own responsibilities to community and family. They are represented as anonymous figures who prepare food, haul wood, tan hides, and take care of children. Only occasionally—outside of official government reports—do Indian women receive any attention as members of their society. These accounts usually come from non-Indian men and women who experience direct contact with an Indian culture. In official reports and other historical pieces written in ignorance of Indian cultures, women are portrayed only in relationship to men—both Indian and non-Indian—as captives, wives, or *squaws*, the Algonquian word for a married or mature woman that later became a demeaning term for all Indian women, Algonkian or not.

Both Indian men and women have been stereotyped to some degree because of an incomplete representation of Indian cultures in written accounts. According to early American history, the Indians played the roles of protector and hostess, ensuring that the Europeans who came to Jamestown and Plymouth Rock survived the winter and successfully settled in North America. Pocahontas and Squanto are particularly important figures of this time.

After the early period of white settlement, Indians are not mentioned in history texts until the so-called settling of the frontier and the last great Indian

An engraving of man, woman, and child of the Naudowelsie, published in part II of Carver's
Travels *(1766–68). Historically, Indian women have been portrayed as caretakers, but rarely
have they been represented in their roles as traders, farmers, artisans, and healers.*

wars of the mid-19th century, when
Crazy Horse, Geronimo, and Sitting
Bull suddenly appear on the scene.

Individual achievement is often
what gets recorded for posterity, and
usually the subjects of such accounts
are male. Recently revised and mod-
ernized textbooks show more sensitiv-
ity to the Indians' diverse and complex
history, and more attention is now
given to some female Indians. However, historical representation of such
figures is still fairly rare and inconse-
quential. At best, Americans know the

names of a few famous American Indian women, such as Pocahontas, Sa-
cagawea, Maria Tallchief, or Maria
Martinez. To people of specific regions
or generations, certain individuals may
be well known. For instance, western-
ers may recognize Sarah Winnemucca's
name, and fans of 1960s music may be
familiar with Buffy St. Marie.

Americans have a very limited
knowledge and understanding of Indians not only because of inadequate
school textbooks but also because of
the inaccurate images presented in lit-

erature, the cinema, and television. For example, the "squaws" of the 19th-century dime novels and in 20th-century movies have helped promote stereotypes: Indian women tend to play an insubstantial role relative to men in ensuring the survival of their culture. When Indian women appear in literature or in movies, their role is often demeaning and negative. They are neither accurately portrayed nor given adequate historical representation.

In the last 10 years, historians have tried to discover more about native women—about their lives, their roles within their society, and their place in American history as a whole. Scholars of American Indian history as well as people in Indian communities seeking to preserve their culture have begun to document on film and in oral histories the lives and stories of native women. Better methods for reconstructing the past as well as the increasing desire to understand the lives of Indian women have helped uncover much information on the Indian population's "hidden half."

Another very important source of information is oral tradition, taken from Indian and non-Indian sources. Some call this material "folklore"; others call it religious narrative. As in any religious narrative that outsiders call "myth," kernels of truth about a culture exist in such stories. These tales, particularly those that are presently alive and flourishing, offer another way of confirming information about the way Indian women see themselves and how they are viewed and understood within their own culture.

In addition, historians can make use of paintings, drawings, and photographs of Indians by non-Indians and of objects old and new that have long been made and used by Indians to gather facts about their ways of life. Although ancient Indian objects have been excavated and interpreted by non-Indian scholars, Indians who know and understand their people's history are increasingly lending their interpretation of archaeological evidence to history.

The written record is of course an important source of information when reconstructing any history. But for a long time it was provided by outsiders who were male and non-Indian, such as missionaries, diplomats, traders, and explorers; thus, much of it was biased. Therefore, historians have to examine the sources of such information and ask what interests and opinions the "informer" might have had. A Christian missionary, for example, would have had a very different notion of polygamy—the marriage of a person to more than one spouse at the same time—than those who actually practiced it.

Indian history told from an Indian point of view could, of course, also be accused of bias. Therefore, in order to form the most complete picture of American history, all sides must be viewed. Thus, when writing on the life of Indian women, historians not only should utilize data provided by non-Indians; they should also seek to un-

An ad from the early 20th century for Wildroot Dandruff Remedy. Advertising, as well as literature, the cinema, and television, has perpetuated stereotypes of Indians. Two prevailing images of native women in American culture have been the kind, beautiful Princess and the violent, filthy "squaw."

LONG DIVISION: A TRIBAL HISTORY
Wendy Rose (Hopi/Miwok)

Our skin loosely lies
across grass borders;
stones loading up
are loaded down with placement sticks,
a great tearing
and appearance of holes.
We are bought and divided
into clay pots; we die
on granite scaffolding
on the shape of the Sierras
and lie down with lips open
thrusting songs on the world.
Who are we and do we
still live? The doctor,
asleep, says no.
So outside of eternity
we struggle until our blood
has spread off our bodies
and frayed the sunset edges.
It's our blood that gives you
those southwestern skies.
Year after year we give,
harpooned with hope, only to fall
bouncing through the canyons,
our songs decreasing
with distance.
I suckle coyotes
and grieve.

derstand how an Indian society viewed its women. Also, perhaps in writing from an Indian point of view, history should be presented in time frames more relevant to the Indians' experience.

Most non-Indians see the history of the Americas as beginning with the arrival of white men. Indian groups, however, had their own ways of marking historical events. For example, what historians refer to as Pre-Columbian America, or America before the coming of Europeans, has no specific time reference for Indian peoples in general. Each Indian group had its own sense of time periods, names for those periods, and an understanding of what each one meant. They kept their own calendar and had their own way to measure the passage of time.

The Indians' experience after the arrival of whites receives only secondary consideration in non-Indian American history. One terribly important period in Indian history is the Removal Era, a tragic time when great effort was expended by the U.S. government to remove (relocate) Indians to remote reservations so that whites could settle on traditional Indian land. But American history written by non-Indians usually refers to this time as the triumphant Frontier period.

Similarly, certain periods that represent an era of a specific government policy toward Indians—such as the assimilation and civilization policies—have no exact equivalents in mainstream historical periodization. For Indians, much of the 1930s and 1940s is known as the Reform Era, a period of intense government reform of its Indian policy. Mainstream history refers to these eras as the Great Depression and the war years.

Black Plume, a Blood Indian of the Blackfoot Nation, poses with his two wives in 1892. Polygamy deviated from the customs of the white, male Christians who recorded history. Such practices were often vilified in, if not completely left out of, the written record. Similarly, the respect with which Indian societies treated women has been misrepresented by mainstream historians.

There are also periods in history that are equally significant to both Indians and non-Indians. The two factions may have experienced the same historical event and now view the period in similar ways. However, such episodes are probably significant to Indians in other ways as well. World War II and the 1960s, for example, were important periods of time to all Americans, but the war years were a time in which Indians experienced a great change in their way of life. The sixties, for non-Indian Americans, are thought of as the Kennedy years or the time of hippies, Vietnam, and student rebellions. Mainstream Americans also share the perspective of many American "minority" peoples that the period was the coming of age of civil rights, a time of Black,

Brown, and Red Power. For Indians, the period was also significant because it was a time of tribal nationalism and pan-Indian, or cross-tribal, action.

Undoubtedly, Indian history following the arrival of Europeans should be discussed in terms of the Indians' experience, and a variety of sources should be consulted in gathering information. Moreover, in constructing a history of Indian women in both American Indian and non-Indian societies, it is imperative that writers not concentrate their discussion on individual women who have achieved notoriety. Historians should give full consideration to Indian women as individuals and as a group, portraying them within their own culture before and after contact with non-Indians. ▲

A Navajo sandpainting of Father Sky and Mother Earth surrounded by Rainbow Girl, a symbol of protection. Female spirits central to Indians' lives were often positive figures, indicating the reverence many Indian societies had for women.

A LOOK
AT THEIR
TRADITIONAL ROLES

Stories handed down through many generations reveal much about the beliefs, values, and laws of a particular culture. The roles that women play in these stories indicate to some extent how a society views its women. For example, many Indian tribes believe that their origin as a culture stems from the female. In contrast, people from the Judeo-Christian tradition believe in a singular male deity. Moreover, women in Indian creation stories and female spirits central to everyday life are viewed in a positive light. Contrary to Eve, who collaborates with a serpent to expose man to evil, woman is viewed as the source of life, providing sustenance and protection as well as certain cultural values, such as truth.

The female figures in Indian creation stories are many and varied. The Cherokee say they came from Corn Mother, or Selu, who cut open her breast so that corn could spring forth, giving life to the people. For the Tewa Pueblo people, the first mothers were known as Blue Corn Woman, the summer mother, and White Corn Maiden, the winter mother. The Iroquois believe that they were born into this world from the mud on the back of the Earth, known as Grandmother Turtle. The essentials of life—corn, beans, and squash—were given to them by the Three Sisters. The Iroquois refer to the Three Sisters when giving thanks for food in everyday prayers. The Apache believe that they are descendants of Child of the Water, who was kept safe by his mother, White-Painted Woman, so that he could slay all the monsters and make the world safe for the Apache people. They pray to both White-Painted Woman and Child of the Water. For the Sioux, White Buffalo Calf Woman gave the people the gift of the Pipe, and thus a gift of Truth.

Many other tribes, however, were as male centered as the Europeans that invaded them. These groups had male

21

gods and spirits and placed great importance on male-focused behavior, such as warfare and hunting. Even so, they recognized the importance of women to their society. Beverly Hungry Wolf, a Blackfoot woman, tells a modern version of a story about how men came to live with and depend on women:

> By the time Napi [the first male human] came over to this side of the ocean the Creator had already made more people. . . . But the women couldn't get along with the men, so Napi sent them away in different groups. Not long after, he got together with the chief of the women so that they could decide about some important things. The chief of the women told Napi that he could make the first decision, as long as she could

have the final word. . . . The old people say that ever since then it has been this way between men and women.

According to this story, Napi makes many decisions affecting both women and men, but the chief of the women countermands them, showing that women are more skillful than men. Napi has separated men and women, but the chief of the women decides that they should live together.

> Now at that time men were living real pitiful lives. The clothes they were wearing were made from stiff furs and hides. They couldn't make moccasins or lodges and they couldn't even keep themselves clean. They were nearly starved . . . they were very anxious to join the women.

The female members of the Blackfoot Indians' Matoki Society, posing in ceremonial dress at the Blood Indian Reserve in Alberta, Canada, in the late 19th century. Although a male-centered tribe, the Blackfoot recognized the importance of women to their society and welcomed their participation in public life.

GRANDMOTHER
Paula Gunn Allen (Laguna/Sioux/Lebanese)

Out of her own body she pushed
silver thread, light, air
and carried it carefully on the dark, flying
where nothing moved.

Out of her body she extruded
shining wire, life, and wove the light
on the void.

From beyond time,
beyond oak trees and bright clear water flow,
she was given the work of weaving the strands
of her body, her pain, her vision
into creation, and the gift of having created,
to disappear.

After her,
the women and the men weave blankets into tales of life,
memories of light and ladders,
infinity-eyes, and rain.
After her I sit on my laddered rain-bearing rug
and mend the tear with string.

Although some male-centered societies held their women in high esteem, the peoples who practiced female-centered religions not only revered their women and treated them with respect but also placed a great deal of responsibility in their hands. In the Southeast and Northeast, prior to the arrival of Europeans, Indian groups often had female rulers, although in most instances, whether male or female, Indian rulers were not allowed to wield the kind of absolute power enjoyed by European monarchs. Many accounts from early European explorers and travelers tell of Queens who were significant personages in their tribe. However, there now exists little evidence as to the extent of their rule, powers, or authority.

Although in many tribes women were not the public representatives of their group, they may have taken part in making decisions concerning trade with other peoples. From the Southeast to the West and down through Mexico there operated an extensive trade network in which women participated.

Every tribal group had a different form of social organization. In most, a woman resigned herself to a marriage arranged by her father, brothers, or uncles, but she retained control over her own body and behavior, over her children, and over the property she held prior to matrimony or had produced during the marriage. In many groups, divorce was common and relatively easy. Usually, women simply moved back to their family's dwelling or asked their husband to take his belongings and leave. In general, whereas a woman was not chattel in Indian societies, in some senses she was just such a slave in European societies.

In many ways, however, Indian women were vulnerable members of society. They needed to rely on a man to hunt for them and otherwise provide what women could not. If a woman lost her male provider through divorce, marriage, or death, another male would have to take his place. Often, for example, a man might marry his wife's widowed or divorced sister in order to provide for her and improve his own household's ability to provide for relatives.

In many of the northeastern, southeastern, and southwestern tribes, women enjoyed a great deal of power and authority within their family. These tribes were usually matrilocal, meaning that when a man and woman married, they took up residence near the female partner's family. The groups also tended to be matrilineal: Children were born into, and received their identity from, their mother's family, and they traced their lineage through their

mother. The inheritance of personal property and the right to hold office were traced through the female line as well. Women held authority over property and its uses and over the disposition of material goods that came from their own work as well as that of men. The distribution of food and other resources was their responsibility.

A group of family members who have a shared identity and property and trace their descent from a common ancestor is called a *clan*. For the female-centered Iroquois and Cherokee, every clan had a clan mother who nominated and deposed chiefs and subchiefs, those hereditary and nonhereditary male leaders who conducted the business of governance. Women joined men in councils and functioned as representatives of women and children. Mothers of those slain in battle and the clan mothers held sway over prisoners and could intervene in the conduct of war and peace.

Although women usually did not take up arms and go into combat, there are numerous stories of women rushing onto the battlefield to protect or substitute for their fallen husbands or brothers. In many instances, they were later given the privilege of fighting or they earned war titles that gave them the privilege of singing and dancing with warriors forever after.

During warfare, women as well as children often fell into the hands of enemy tribes that enslaved their captives. However, rape and sexual aggression against women, including those cap-

A Navajo mother with twins in New Mexico during the late 19th century. In matrilineal societies such as the Navajo's, the inheritance of property and the right to hold office are traced through the female line.

Sioux Indian Minnie Hollow Wood, shown in a photograph taken in 1927, was at one time the only woman in her tribe entitled to wear a warbonnet. She earned this right by taking part in combat against the U.S. cavalry.

tured, does not appear by any account to have been an element of most native cultures. Even white women testified to this feature of native societies in the many documented accounts of captivity that accompanied the first 200 years of contact between Indians and Europeans.

The story of Mary Jemison, a white woman who was captured by the Seneca when she was 15, became one of the most popular and important of the captivity narratives. From Jemison, much has been learned about what life was like for Iroquois women of the late 18th and early 19th century. She lived among the Seneca for 65 years, telling her story when she was 80. After being taken captive, Jemison was renamed and adopted by Seneca women as a surrogate for a brother who had been killed in battle—a common way in which native people dealt with captives.

Jemison said that the women treated her as a real sister, "the same as though I had been born of their mother." Mary described her life with a Delaware husband and her five children as pleasant. Of labor, she said the Indian woman's daily tasks were "probably not harder than that of white women . . . and their cares certainly are not half as numerous, not as great . . . we planted, tended, and harvested our corn, and generally had all our children with us; but had no master to oversee or drive us, so that we could work as leisurely as we pleased."

Among Indian women's most significant roles, both to their family and to the Europeans who ventured to the Americas, was that of agricultural scientist. In 1788, Governor Clinton of New York heard and had his scribes record a speech by Domine Pater, a Seneca-Cayuga orator, made on behalf of his people.

Our ancestors considered it a great offence to reject the counsels of their women, particularly [that] of female governesses. They were esteemed the mistresses of the soil [as they attend to the labours of agriculture]. Who, said they, bring us into being? Who cultivates our land, kindles our fires [or administers food to the calls of the hungry], but our women?

Not only were women in most tribes responsible for gathering and cultivating plants; they also were responsible for developing all the extraordinary varieties of vegetables and fruits used by Indian peoples. Among these were corn, beans, squash, potatoes, peanuts, peppers, sunflowers, tomatoes, and plants from which dyes and medicines were made. Some of these plants make up many of the major food crops in the world today.

Women throughout the Indian world possessed knowledge about everyday health care, though in some tribes women were acknowledged spiritual leaders. Spiritual leaders were primarily male, and many were healers in the sense that they administered spiritual and physical medicine. Women, however, were often respon-

In Montana's Glacier National Park during the late 19th century, Blackfoot Indians sit within a medicine lodge and smoke a pipe before proceeding with ceremonies. Although spiritual leaders in most Indian societies were male, the women were often the healers.

After building a frame and covering it with animal hide, these two Hidatsa women trim the edges of their new boat. In many tribes, in the past as well as today, the women are among the most skilled craftspeople.

sible for treating minor ailments and served as medical consultants for their people. Because they knew about plants, they could prepare herbal medicines and determine what foods were best for an ill person. They devised various treatments for particular ailments or conditions. They were also midwives, taking care of pregnant women and their infants.

Those who feed and nurture the people are indeed valued members of any society. But also treasured are those who have an eye to imagine, design, and construct useful material objects, such as shelters and various types of boats. Inuit artist Pitseolak explains in a 1971 autobiography that her family made long and dangerous hunting journeys "in sealskin boats, which were wooden frames covered with sealskins. They used to be called the women's boats because they were sewn by the women." Honored as well, both then and now, were the women who constructed houses for their family—hogans for the Navajo, the wickiup for the Apache, the tipis for Plains people, the chickees for the Seminole. In Pueblo society, the women made mud into bricks and built adobes, replastering these mud houses every year. In the past as well as today, women are skilled craftspeople, producing beautiful, essential objects for decoration, everyday or ceremonial use, and exchange.

Unfortunately, much of the rich and complex history of early native women will never be known. Neither they nor Indian men—with the exception of a few societies, such as the Aztec—committed their tales to a retrievable record. Information must be deduced from a society's origin story or from other tales of the Indians' past life. But even this information from early times is flawed, because Indian women most often were not in control of their own stories. History was often filtered through the eyes and sensibilities of non-Indian men, who possessed potentially biased visions.

Later, in the early and mid-20th century, some Indian women's tales were collected by scholars, such as Gilbert Wilson and Nancy Lurie, who were taken into native communities and lived as family members with the people about whom they wrote. Often, however, when Indian women began to speak for themselves, their stories were intruded upon by "friendly interpreters" who translated material incorrectly. Increasingly, however, women have begun to tell their stories as they wish, drawing upon the multiple perspectives—both traditional and non-Indian—that have shaped their life. ▲

Helen Goes Ahead, a woman of the Crow tribe. Because warriors made a practice of capturing women from the opposing camp, the Blackfoot and the Crow, once archenemies, are now interrelated. Both Indian and European men treated Indian women as objects. However, Indian tribes often accepted captives into their communities, whereas the Europeans usually enslaved them.

THE INVASION
OF
THE AMERICAS

In what is now the southwestern United States, native peoples experienced direct contact with Europeans as early as 1540. Initially, these people were more fortunate than the natives of Mexico and South America, who earlier had been cruelly exploited by Spanish conquistadors. To the north, the Spanish tended to respect the rights of Indians to their land and granted them legal title to it. Even so, as revealed by Spanish intellectual Juan Genes de Sepulveda in 1547, the conquistadors thought of Indians as inferiors and aimed to control them, as well as the riches of their land. In comparing the conquerors with the conquered, Sepulveda wrote that "if you know the customs and the nature of the two people, . . . with perfect right the Spaniards rule over these barbarians of the New World and the adjacent lands; who in wisdom, virtue, intelligence and humanitas are as inferior to the Spaniards as infants to adults and women to men."

The intruders demanded the Indians' food stores, goods, and labor. Soon they also began forcing Indians to cede land on which they wished to settle. They also initiated policies intended to compel Indians to abandon many of their traditional practices. From the very beginning, Indian people resisted European imperialism, but the damage that contact with whites had inflicted on Indian culture was irreparable.

Many Indians living in other areas of North America were hurt by the presence of non-Indians before actually meeting the strangers from across the ocean. The Europeans had brought with them diseases, such as smallpox and measles, that had previously been unknown in the New World. Because Indians had not developed immunity to these European germs, the first peoples to have contact with whites readily contracted the unfamiliar diseases and spread them to other Indian groups. Epidemics traveled northward from South America and the Caribbean, killing many thousands of people and devastating whole communities. In the first 200 years after the European invasion of North America, somewhere between 8 million and 20 million native peoples died. Many tribal groups were entirely wiped out.

In the Northeast, native people first experienced direct contact with Europeans in the early 17th century, when French explorers traveled down the St. Lawrence River. Soon after, the French established a network of trade alliances with various Indian tribes. French trad-

Widows Lamenting the Dead, a 17th-century engraving by Theodore de Bry of Timucua Indians and Spanish conquistadores. In the first 200 years after Europeans invaded the Americas, war and disease killed somewhere between 8 million and 20 million native peoples.

ers often enlisted Indian aid and adopted native customs, such as that of exchanging gifts. The British, however, came to North America primarily to trade and to farm. As they founded colonies, they drove the Indians out.

By the early 17th century, French fur traders had moved into the Great Lakes region, and the Dutch had built a trading post near present-day Albany, New York. The Dutch began trading firearms to the Indians. As competition for European goods intensified between tribes, so did armed warfare, and casualties increased. After the British succeeded the Dutch at Albany in the late 17th century, French and British traders became fierce competitors. Also, as French colonists moved southward from present-day Canada, they came into conflict with British settlers moving westward from the coast. Indian tribes that had established trade relations with either the French or British participated in the continual armed conflict between the two groups.

In the mid-18th century, after the British secured a victory over the French in the French and Indian War (1754–63), British military commanders and settlers began moving into areas surrendered by France. Indians living in the Great Lakes region along the Ohio River were threatened by white settlement. Many tribes joined forces under the leadership of Pontiac and captured British forts west of the Appalachians. The Indians failed to run the whites out of their territory, but the strength and solidarity of the Indian

forces prompted the British to establish a boundary line beyond which no settlers could pass until the British government negotiated treaties with the Indians. White settlers, however, continued to pour into the Indians' territory, and new conflicts ensued.

After the invasion of North America, Indian women's lives, like those of their male counterparts, changed immediately. Of course, death from disease was blind to gender, but in other ways the coming of Europeans to the Americas affected women differently than it did men. The economic, political, and social status of the former suffered immeasurably.

One of the first casualties was the overt and important participation of many women in the leadership of Indian peoples. Europeans often simply refused to negotiate with or recognize female leaders. As indicated by Sepulveda, to the Europeans, women were to men as infants were to adults. Even though many Europeans were accustomed to rule by female monarchs (e.g., Isabella I of Spain and Elizabeth I of England), the Europeans who first came to the Americas were men who preferred to deal only with men.

At first, Indian men who were used to the active participation of women in councils were surprised at the absence of women from European decision making. In one well-known story from the early 18th century, Outacitty (also known as Ostenaco) led a Cherokee delegation to meet British representatives. His first words upon meeting the

An early-19th-century sketch by Peter Rindisbacher of a Cree family that lived and hunted near the Hudson's Bay Company trading post. As Indians became dependent on European goods, they began to ally themselves with the whites with whom they traded. Later, these bonds turned into military alliances when Europeans began to war among themselves in North America.

British were "Where are your women?" The British, of course, were surprised by Outacitty's inquiry; in their society, women did not participate in important affairs of state and certainly not in military delegations.

Repeatedly, French and English missionaries and diplomats tried to negate the presence and power of women by refusing to negotiate with them. In 1762, Kanadiohora, a Seneca, informed Sir William Johnson that he was to come and speak to him on official business at the request of the Seneca women. Johnson asked that women not attend the council, as was their custom. Kanadiohora replied that "it was always the Custom for [women] to be present at

Such Occasions (being of Much Estimation Amongst Us, in that we proceed from them and they provide our Warriors with Provisions when they go abroad), they were therefore Resolved to come down."

Johnson persisted in his opposition to the participation of both the warriors and the women in council meetings with the British, insisting that the chiefs alone attend. Ironically, Johnson was himself later married to an Indian woman, the sister of Mohawk leader Joseph Brant. Molly Brant's importance to her people brought Johnson great influence among the Indians.

Likewise, as the wife of an Englishman, Molly Brant enjoyed the kind of status known to few Indian women after contact with Europeans: For the most part, Indian women were not only excluded from decision making but also were victims of open violence and aggression. They were often captured and forced to submit to humiliating treatment. Many were raped.

The central myth of the European conquest of the Americas is embodied in the story of Pocahontas. The legend of Pocahontas holds that her father, Chief Powhatan, ordered the death of Captain John Smith, one of the founders of the English colony of Jamestown. Supposedly, Pocahontas threw her body over Smith the moment before his execution and convinced her father to spare the Englishman's life. From a European perspective, Pocahontas was a good native woman who saved a good

white man from her evil and violent relatives. But the story was far from the truth and certainly not representative of the early encounters between Indian women and white men.

According to the Indians' account, John Smith, as the leader of the English company, was chosen by Powhatan to be adopted into the chief's family. As the daughter of the tribe's leader and a woman of considerable status, Pocahontas served as Smith's "mother," for he had to be reborn, after a symbolic death, as one of the tribe. Thus, Pocahontas was not delaying Smith's execution and thwarting her own people when she threw her body over his. She was in fact acting on behalf of her people. From the Indians' perspective, Pocahontas formed a bond between them and the English by giving life— symbolically—to John Smith.

Although European men romanticized early encounters with Indian women, sexual violence became a major problem for Indian women after the arrival of the Spanish, French, and British. Fighting often broke out between natives and Europeans because native men tried to protect or hide women from marauding soldiers and adventurers, who often took more than food stores, furs, and gold from Indian villages. Accounts given by the Spanish themselves tell of women being lassoed like cattle and dragged off. The men who tried to stop them were shot. Often soldiers killed Indian men in order to take their wives and daughters. Such depredations gave rise to reprisals by Indians, which in turn prompted retaliation by the Europeans.

Early on, some Europeans, such as the friars who had been sent to convert the Indians to Christianity, begged their governments to find a means of restraining European soldiers and men from abusing, attacking, capturing, and raping native women. How could they spread Christianity, they asked, if they were continually faced with soldiers who relished the very acts of fornication, rape, and sexual impurity that Christians were not supposed to commit? Although the Spanish eventually tried to reward men who married Christianized Indians by giving them land, animals, and other resources, the sexual violence continued.

Women and children had been treated as objects for trade by certain Indian societies. When Europeans arrived, this activity not only continued but actually intensified. Various groups of Europeans began to extend special

Smith Rescued by Pocahontas, *an engraving made in the 19th century. In what became the central myth of the conquest of the Americas, Pocahontas is said to have saved John Smith from her evil and violent relatives. Actually, Smith's supposed execution was part of an adoption ritual, and Pocahontas was acting as his "mother" during this ceremony by giving him a new birth into her tribe.*

favors to those Indians that brought them slaves from other tribes. Although both whites and Indians treated women and children as commercial items, Indian tribes often accepted a captive into the community, where the captive would marry or be adopted by a member of the tribe.

Large numbers of women who were captured, stolen, and sold to Europeans became servants and sexual partners. They rarely became wives and children of white men. Even as late as the late 19th century, such enslavements, though less common, were still taking place. A Navajo woman living during this period told her children and grandchildren of her repeated capture by the Apache and the Ute as well as by a cavalry troop in which she served as the "wife" of a soldier until she was able to escape and return to Navajo country. With the Apache and the Ute, she was not a sexual servant; with the U.S. cavalry, she was.

Whether by force or consent, European men and Indian women began having sexual relations. As soon as Europeans arrived, the number of native women in present-day Canada and the United States who married or stayed with fur traders in the forts and towns grew in number. Traders and observers felt that the women were better off. From their perspective, an Indian woman had fewer responsibilities as the wife of a trader; she was not expected to work to support herself, her children, or her other relatives. She probably also enjoyed a better, more

consistent supply of food and goods not produced by her own labor.

However, an Indian woman allied to a fur trader had less control over her life and the lives of the children she bore from her white partner; apparently, women married to whites gave birth to more children. She could not divorce of her own free will, and the goods and dwelling that might have been her own property in Indian society became the possession of her white husband.

Marital alliances, made for various reasons by Indians and Europeans, were often temporary and resulted in misunderstanding. In some tribes, adult women were free to seek out sexual alliances with whomever they

THE BLANKET AROUND HER
Joy Harjo (Creek)

maybe it is her birth
which she holds close to herself
or her death
which is just as inseparable
and the white wind
that encircles her is a part
just as
    the blue sky
hanging in turquoise from her neck

oh woman
remember who you are
woman
it is the whole earth

chose. The children belonged entirely to women, as did the property and distribution of resources. Indian men abided by the rules of society. If a couple separated, the man would leave with only that which had belonged to him when he entered the relationship; if a woman formed an alliance with a European by choice, she had every reason to imagine that her society's rules would be followed. For Indians, a white man who married an Indian was expected to acknowledge the importance and status of women.

Europeans, however, had different notions than did many Indian tribes about inheritance, especially concerning children. In the European mind, marriage gave the male control of the property and of the children. Whites actually exploited the Indian woman's status to further alienate Indians from their property and territory. Many white men married Indian women of status (e.g., the sister of a leader) so that they could then secure a right to her property as well as the friendship of her male relatives. When conflict over property rights inevitably arose, European laws dominated, and the status of women was undermined.

As late as the early 20th century, when oil was discovered in Oklahoma, white men married into wealthy female-centered Osage families and inherited the family's property. Under Osage practice, the oil revenues would have been reserved for the woman's family and controlled by her. Common property laws established by white men

gave the husband control. In a number of notorious instances in Oklahoma, women were murdered so that their husbands could inherit their wealth.

Perhaps, for many women, accepting life with traders, soldiers, and other white men was a way of deferring to the awful reality of the European presence. Women allied to traders and military men, as well as their mixed-blood children, became interpreters and liaisons between Indians and whites. Such a role undoubtedly caused many women and children to feel mixed loyalties, for often they not only were responsible for mediating and preventing hostilities but also betrayed their Indian family.

For the Europeans, Indian women—whether as wives, mistresses, or temporary companions—were a necessity of life in the New World. Whereas ladies of European heritage often did not desire and could not have borne the rough life of the early days on the fur-trade frontier, Indian women actually helped white men survive. For some traders, an alliance with an Indian woman ensured that they would always have food and shelter.

Many traders felt safe in Indian country as long as they were accompanied by an Indian woman of the area. For others, the sexual alliance with an Indian woman was a temporary convenience to be put aside for a white wife when they returned to "civilization." But even when a less arduous and more pleasant life became possible in the forts and border towns, white men often pre-

Josette Legacé, a mixed-blood shown with her daughter Suzette and son David, accompanied her husband on most of his trading expeditions. Even after life became less strenuous in forts and border towns, many white men continued to prefer mixed-blood women as wives.

Through her knowledge of Carrier Indian customs, Amelia Douglas, a mixed-blood, saved the life of her white husband, James Douglas. With the help of Indian women, many white men who might otherwise have perished were able to survive and even thrive during the early days on the fur-trade frontier.

ferred mixed-blood women as wives. There are substantial accounts of long-term marriages between such partners.

Many trappers and traders actually maintained two families—one Indian and one white. Such practices, especially when the relationships between white men and native women were not legalized through formal marriage, caused great difficulties not only for In-dian women and their families but for the white friends and families of the men.

Such arrangements were probably considered appropriate in the West, but if women and children were brought east, they encountered a world that abhorred racial mixing. By the mid-19th century, the Indian population had grown so small in the East that most whites had never been exposed to Indians except through sensational accounts. Although mixing with the Indians was actually thought by some to be the key to "civilizing" them, white men who consorted with Indian women were called "squawmen." Missionaries attacked the frontier custom of marrying without benefit of formal services and fought against mixed-blood marriages.

Unlike most Indian tribes, in which people from other cultures were often adopted and treated like those born into the group, Europeans were suspicious of other peoples. As more and more whites flooded into the formerly "uncivilized" country in the West during the 19th century, racial prejudice became a fact of daily life and made mixed racial unions more difficult. Sexual unions that were once seen as necessary to the "civilization" of the savage became morally scandalous.

The children of racially mixed marriages came to be a despised race. Persons of mixed Indian, white, and, in some instances, African heritage were thought of and treated differently than their full-blooded white relatives. In

In this pencil sketch (ca. 1825) by Peter Rindisbacher of an Indian man and his two mixed-blood wives, the women wear nontraditional clothing, including high-waisted gowns with low bodices and skirts that almost reach their ankles. The creation of mixed-blood populations, as well as the introduction of European goods and customs to the New World, changed forever the nature of Indian cultures.

some instances, a bloodline that included white genes elevated a person's status from that of other Indians or Africans. But having a mixed heritage also caused some to lose status.

The conquest of the Indians was accomplished not by war. Fighting between Indians and Europeans was only in part responsible for the demise of Indian cultures. Disease and demoral-

ization killed millions, but the sexual conquest of North America actually secured a cultural victory over native peoples. The creation of an enormous mixed-blood population changed forever the nature of Indian societies, prompting debates among many who are today concerned with the persistence, and the very definition, of Indian cultures. ▲

The Trail of Tears, *painted by Robert Lindneux in 1942, depicts the arduous journey made by the Cherokee during the winter of 1839 in present-day Oklahoma. Even before whites forced the Indians from their homeland, they changed the Cherokee's systems of trade and governance, which traditionally included the active participation of women.*

THE TOLLS
OF
"CIVILIZATION"

After the colonists gained their independence from Great Britain in the American Revolution, their new central government—called the Confederation Congress—created the Indian Department, which was responsible for regulating trade with the Indians and managing affairs with those tribes living in unsettled areas from the Appalachian Mountains to the Mississippi River. In the 1780s, the Indian Department began negotiating treaties with the Indians, forcing them to cede their vast land to the United States without direct compensation in favor of small reserves that the government guaranteed "as long as the grass shall grow and the waters flow."

Native peoples had already endured great hardships and deprivations as a result of continual warfare on the continent. Many had already lost their homeland to white settlers. By 1795, Indians living north of the Ohio River, in the Northwest Territory, had ceded most of what is now central and southern Ohio and had given the United States the right to buy the remainder of their lands north of the Ohio River and east of the Mississippi.

After Thomas Jefferson purchased the Louisiana Territory in 1803, he encouraged tribes living south of the Ohio River, including the Cherokee, Creek, Choctaw, and Chickasaw, to move farther west. However, unlike the Indians in the Northwest Territory, those tribes living in the middle and southern United States saw no reason to give up their land. They were prosperous, settled farmers who had been at peace with the U.S. government.

Although Jefferson put no further pressure on the Indians to cede their land, many tribes feared that the U.S. government would eventually force them to move west. When the United States and Great Britain once again

43

went to war, tribes in the Northeast joined British forces and attacked American settlements. A victory over the British and the Indians in the War of 1812 shifted the balance of power in favor of the United States, and many tribes in the Northeast were forced to abandon their homes and move westward into Louisiana Territory. Tribes in the South were able to hold off the government for a while longer, arguing that they had already signed treaties that guaranteed their right to the land.

Before the white men had arrived, the Cherokee were dominant in the present-day states of Georgia, North and South Carolina, Tennessee, and Virginia. They had a system of government in which leadership roles were awarded to both men and women. Nanyehi had earned her title as governor of the Women's Council and the last Beloved Woman of the Cherokee after showing great leadership during a war against the Creek Indians. She could speak for women on matters of peace and war and domestic policy.

When white men first came into Cherokee territory and established new systems of trade and economic behavior, many tribe members believed that native peoples could not peacefully coexist with these predatory people and that no amount of appeasement would ever be sufficient to stop them from completely annihilating Indians. Nanyehi believed that in order to survive it was necessary to accommodate the intruders and to befriend them. She continually intervened on behalf of whites when they encroached upon Cherokee territory. After her Cherokee husband, Kingfisher, died, Nanyehi married Irish trader Brian Ward and became known to whites as Nancy Ward.

During the American Revolution, when the colonies revolted, the Cherokees sided with the British, and their lands and goods were devastated. In an attempt to save what was left of their possessions, the tribe decided to sign a peace treaty, giving the United States the right to regulate trade with the Indians and to manage their affairs. At the peace council in 1785, Nanyehi presented strings of shell beads called wampum on behalf of the Women's Council as a show of goodwill and mutual obligation to commissioners.

For a while, the Cherokee people lived in relative peace and adopted many ways of the whites who populated their land. In the early 1820s, pressure to do so grew as the U.S. government initiated its "civilization" policy, by which it sought to compel the Indians to forsake their culture and live like whites. The Cherokee conformed to the tenets of the program. Many farmed and sent their children to schools to learn English. But no matter how the Cherokee succeeded in adopting the characteristics of civilization—as whites understood it—more and more settlers arrived wanting to remove the Cherokee.

Many Cherokee felt that they should simply relent and relocate to the land west of the Mississippi that the government had designated as Indian

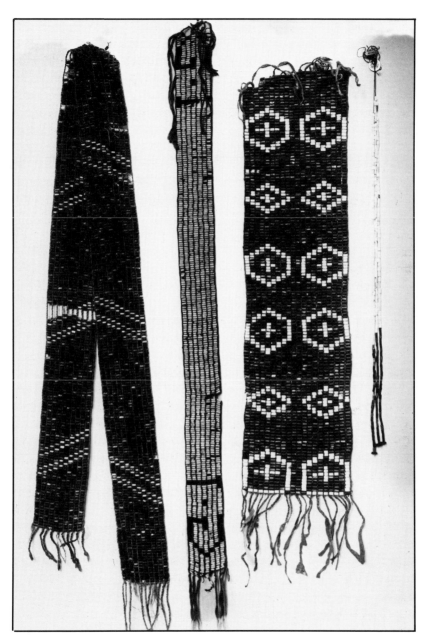

Among eastern tribes, wampum belts, like the peace pipe, were employed in the rituals of diplomacy. The smoking of a peace pipe endowed diplomatic treaty councils with a sense of sacredness, whereas the exchange of wampum symbolized social and political agreements between convening parties.

Territory. But past betrayals instilled distrust in Nanyehi and many others who had once befriended whites. This group experienced a change of heart and refused to leave their homeland, their sacred ground. Although she had vacated her office as Beloved Woman and a new form of government had been adopted by the Cherokee, one that abolished the women's councils and was modeled on white governments, Nanyehi communicated her thoughts and wishes to the council in 1817:

> Cherokee mothers do not wish to go to an unknown country. . . . We have raised all of you on the land which we now inhabit. We have understood that some of our children wish to govern the Mississippi, but this act . . . would be like destroying your mothers. We beg of you not to part with any more of our land.

Even as late as 1825, the Cherokee heeded the counsel of women. At negotiations concerning the proposed removal of the Cherokee to the West, one of the tribe's leaders presented General William Clark with wampum. These strings of shell were brought to show the Indians' desire for peace. One string was described as being from the women, who strongly advised the men "to pursue in our undertaking and not give it up." General Clark, however, no more heeded the advice of Indian women than did his predecessors and some Cherokee men.

In response to the demands of white settlers, the state of Georgia passed legislation in 1827 that extended its authority over Cherokee lands, and Congress passed the Indian Removal Act in 1830, which permitted the president, Andrew Jackson, to negotiate with eastern Indians on their removal to the West. Even though the Cherokee hired lawyers and fought in the courts to protect their homeland, the Indians were strong-armed and forced to surrender their rights to the land. Many conflicts followed, and the Cherokee resisted removal. Eventually, they were driven to Indian Territory in present-day Oklahoma. As many as 6,000 may have died on their Trail of Tears across the Mississippi in the winter of 1838–39, and Nanyehi's beloved homeland was lost forever.

Before the Removal Era, the government policy of "civilizing" the Indians nearly completed the destruction that disease and war had begun. When the conversion of Indians to Christianity—which had long been a goal of the Europeans who colonized the Americas—became part of federal policy, missionaries were encouraged to stake out their claims on Indian souls across the country. Various denominations moved among the Indians and set up mission schools to educate Indian children.

In addition to educating and converting the Indians to Christianity, the government sought to make farmers out of them. European notions deemed that native men would be more settled and tractable if they were torn away from their life as "savage" hunters. In

Missionary Kate McBeth and a group of Nez Perce women (ca. 1889–91). When the conversion of Indians to Christianity became part of federal policy in the early 19th century, missionaries were encouraged to live among various tribes and set up schools and churches.

order to accomplish this goal, the government had to obstruct the established system of production and distribution of resources. Thus, many women not only lost their right to participate in the tribe's government, but they were also deprived of their specialized role as agriculturist.

Whites may have believed such change was for the better where Indian women were concerned. The casual observer failed to realize that the strenuous labors of an Indian woman assured her a great deal of power. Al-

though she worked very hard, she enjoyed control over the products of her labor. Among groups as varied as the Iroquois in the Northeast and the Hidatsa of the Great Northern Plains, the power to trade and distribute the products of agricultural labor resided in the women. Numerous reports from the 19th century clearly indicate that Indian women traded corn, for example, for other goods and supplies. In the 1850s, F. V. Hayden, an agent sent to the Plains to administer government policy there, reported that "though the women perform all this labor, they are compensated by having their full share of the profits."

For the most part, whites writing in the 19th century express a repugnance for Indian women and their work. In 1885, William Clark wrote:

> In savagery and barbarism women are merely beasts of burden, prized and valued for their skill in fancy or capacity for heavy work, rather than for any beauty of face or figure. . . ."

Others wrote of the Indian woman's sexual promiscuity, her state of abso-lute slavery to men, and her seemingly tragic migratory life. It was assumed that hard labor among Indian women existed because of the brutality, immorality, and laziness considered inherent in Indian men. Yet, Indian men acknowledged the need to be good to women, who were an important and powerful force. At the age of 92, He Dog, a Sioux Indian, told anthropologist Marla Powers that "it is well to be good to women in the strength of our manhood because we must sit under their hands at both ends of our lives."

In truth, it was not brutality on the part of Indian men but the contact with

A Hidatsa woman turning the soil in her corn garden with a bone hoe. Among the Hidatsa, as well as many other tribes, the power to trade and distribute products of agricultural labor was held by the women. When the government tried to make farmers out of Indian men, many women were deprived of their role as agriculturists.

WOMANWORK

Paula Gunn Allen (Laguna/Sioux/Lebanese)

some make potteries
some weave and spin
remember
the Woman/celebrate
webs and making
out of own flesh
earth
bowl and urn
to hold water
and ground corn
balanced on heads
and springs lifted
and rivers in our eyes
brown hands shaping
earth into earth
food for bodies
water for fields
they use
old pots
broken
fragments
castaway

bits
to make new
mixed with clay
it makes strong
bowls, jars
new
she
brought
light
we remember this
as we make
the water bowl
broken
marks the grandmother's grave
so she will shape water
for bowls
for food growing
for bodies
eating
at drink
thank her

---

whites that had precipitated an increase in labor among tribes. Trade with whites had increased the amount of work for which women were responsible, because they alone had the skill to tan the hides of deer, elk, and buffalo. It may even have been the case that polygamy, which so repelled whites, actually proliferated as a result of the fur trade. Having more laborers in a family to prepare hides increased revenue, which was clearly necessary to Indian peoples forced to rely on white goods.

Historian Sherry Smith writes that white men and women on the 19th-century frontier—people who were actually in contact with Indians—held conflicting and often irreconcilable views of Indian women. Some felt that "a happier, more lighthearted, more contented woman cannot be found" but that her lightheartedness was due to "ignorance of the alternatives or constant work which kept her from reflecting on the horrors of her life." An army officer wrote that in spite of what he regarded as drudgery, the lives of Indian women were better than the "do-nothing, thankless dyspeptic life led by

In this photo from the late 19th century, two Blackfoot women in Montana prepare a hide. The fur trade made great demands on the Indian woman's specialized skills. Accordingly, the practice of polygamy among some tribes increased, because the more wives a man had, the more revenue his family took in.

a majority of American women." He concluded that this was because of their exercise and outdoor existence.

Many officers recognized that Indian women enjoyed economic, marital, and political privileges unknown to most white women. Some felt that unlike white women who demanded rights, Indian women earned them because they engaged in "manly labor."

Army officers also noted that Indian forms of marriage were advantageous to women, noting that Shawnee and Delaware women could, like their husbands, dissolve the marriage at will and that a woman would retain all the property she possessed at the time of marriage. Army officers' wives, on the other hand, who came into contact with Indian women generally felt and expressed the sentiment that the women were enslaved by their husbands.

In the 19th century, there were two very separate and distinct images of Indian women prevalent among non-Indians in the East. One was of a violent, degraded, and filthy creature—a "squaw." The second was that of the Princess. Like Pocahontas, she was the kind, beautiful daughter of a noble leader. Writers, journalists, and the public in general made these two conflicting images a reality in the mind of most people. Because few non-Indians in the East saw any Indians after the Removal Era, one of the two stereotyped images prevailed.

In the mid-19th century, as white women came west and lived near native peoples, they became friendly with them, particularly with the women. According to journals and diaries, they served as midwives for each other and exchanged information about medicines, health practices, and the preparation of food. White women also began to marry Indian men, and many more Indian women married white men, increasing the mixed-blood population.

As settlers moved west, however, Indians once again faced encroaching whites and broken treaties. Between 1830 and 1850, about 100,000 Indians had moved to what was commonly referred to as the "permanent Indian country" in present-day Oklahoma. In 1848, after the United States had secured the Oregon country and the region stretching from what is now Texas to California, Indian Territory was situated between the sparsely populated land to the west and settlers to the east. In the end, many Indians were chased off land that the U.S. government had, only decades before, promised would be theirs forever. ▲

A Sioux family on Standing Rock Reservation, North Dakota, in 1902. With the opening of the so-called frontier in the mid-19th century, the government negotiated treaties with natives living west of the Mississippi. It also enacted a policy of "civilizing" Western Indians by banning the observation of traditional rituals on reservations and encouraging the practice of Christianity.

RESERVATION LIFE

Since its creation, the U.S. government had forced Indians to cede entire tribal territories in exchange for treaty-based guarantees of personal safety, sovereignty, and rights to water and other resources on small, reserved tracts of land. As the so-called frontier opened up to settlers, the government negotiated more treaties with Indians living west of the Mississippi, particularly with Plains Indians and tribes living in the Southwest.

One Plains group, the Blackfoot Nation, composed of Blackfoot, Piegan, Blood, and Hidatsa Indians, signed a treaty that not only allowed settlers to pass through their land peacefully but also gave the United States full rights to their territory. In return, the Indians were given goods and provisions as well as an annuity (annual payment) from the government. They also could live on their own land as long as they built no permanent settlements. Farther north, the Sioux signed a treaty ceding their lands in Minnesota and Iowa. They were granted a small reservation along the Mississippi River.

Such treaties instilled resentment in the Plains Indians. When troops who had been occupying forts in the West were recalled in 1861 to fight in the Civil War, Plains Indians as well as southwestern tribes took advantage of the opportunity and tried, unsuccessfully, to run whites out of their territory. After the war, the government decided to re-evaluate its Indian policy.

A congressional committee, led by senator James R. Doolittle, investigated conditions in the West and discovered that whites had encroached on Indian lands and had destroyed the buffalo herds on which Plains Indians depended for survival. Because the Indians were weak and vulnerable, the Doolittle committee recommended that all Indians of the Plains be placed on reservations, where they could be protected from whites. By the 1880s, this advice had been followed, and most Indians were confined to relatively small tracts of land.

Although the Doolittle committee had recommended confining Indians for their own protection, the refuge most Indians were provided was in truth a prison. On reservations men could no longer hunt to provide food and clothing. For both women and men, this meant that those responsibilities that once brought them honor and respect were now gone. Women's tanning and quilling societies, for example, became almost obsolete, because trade cloth, instead of animal hide, was used to make clothing.

Even greater change was brought about when non-Indians once again became strongly intent on "civilizing" reservation Indians. Government officials believed that individual land ownership was the key to a speedier assimilation into white culture. In 1887, Congress passed the General Allotment Act, also known as the Dawes Act, which called for reservation land to be divided into small tracts and parceled out to Indians. Because the government believed Indians were too incompetent to manage their own affairs, land was held in trust for 25 years. During this time, Indians could not sell or lease their tracts without the government's

Arapaho women performing the Ghost Dance (ca. 1893). After Congress passed the General Allotment Act in 1887, Indians who were beset by feelings of helplessness and the prospect of total cultural disintegration began practicing this new religion. Combining old spiritual beliefs with Christianity, the Ghost Dance promised that whites would disappear from their lands.

CALLING MYSELF HOME
Linda Hogan (Chickasaw)

There were old women
who lived on amber.
Their dark hands
laced the shells of turtles
together, pebbles inside
and they danced
with rattles strong on their legs.

There is a dry river
between them and us.
Its banks divide up our land.
Its bed was the road
I walked to return.

We are plodding creatures
like the turtle
born of an old people.
We are nearly stone
turning slow as the earth.
Our mountains are underground
they are so old.

This land is the house
we have always lived in.
The women,
their bones are holding up the earth.
The red tail of a hawk
cuts open the sky
and the sun
brings their faces back
with the new grass.

Dust from yarrow
is in the air,
the yellow sun.
Insects are clicking again.

I came back to say good-bye
to the turtle
to those bones
to the shells locked together
on his back,
gold atoms dancing underground.

---

permission. Corrupt federal management allowed the leasing and sale—all at bargain prices for the non-Indian buyer and leaseholder—of millions of acres of prime land. Throughout the next 100 years, most Indian lands would be alienated from individuals and tribes. Some lands are still held "in trust."

The government also banned the performance of traditional ceremonies, songs, and dances in its attempt to assimilate Indians. At the turn of the 20th century, anthropologists and historians began to interview many of the women who lived through these changes. The women described their traditional life, how that life changed when the whites came to their land, and how they tried to continue to observe the old ways. Ruth Underhill, an anthropologist, commented on what she had observed in Pueblo society in the Southwest in the 1920s and what Pueblo women had told her of traditional ceremonial life and of women's roles in it. She learned of ceremonies called deer dances, which were intended to bring in game. As described by the Pueblo women,

> men wore deerskins and danced for the hunters and the game. In their midst was a beautiful Pueblo woman with long black hair, in all the regalia of white boots and embroidered manta. She was their owner, the Mother of the Game. But she was also Earth Mother, the source of all live things—including men. She led the animals where they would be good targets for the hunters, and one by one, they were symbolically killed.

On reservations, after the government had banned ceremonies, women's roles, like those of the men, in the ritual life of their community were forever changed. Women who had once been central to their tribe's rituals experienced a diminution in social status. In Sioux society, for example, women could no longer sponsor the Sun Dance or a vision quest. Female and male elders, once respected in traditional culture for their wisdom and guidance, found themselves held in low esteem by those of a European worldview. The medicines and ceremonial skills they had known so well were reviled as quirks of savagery. Little wonder that men, and later many women, turned to suicide and alcohol in despair.

Even with the continued assault on their culture, some Indian people tried not to abandon their old way of life. In the Hidatsa world, before the time of reservations, women's societies played

vital roles in the life of the people. Members of the Goose Society performed ceremonies in order to make the corn crop prosper, and, like the Sioux, the White Buffalo Cow women danced to attract the buffalo. Anthropologist Gilbert Wilson recorded the story of one Hidatsa woman, named Waheenee, or Buffalo Bird Woman, who lived from 1840 to the 1930s. She described to him the Hidatsa way of life before white people intruded on tribal land and moved her people away from their homes:

> My father's lodge, or better, my mother's lodge—for an earth lodge belonged to the women who built it— was more carefully constructed than most winter lodges. . . . I learned to cook deer skins, embroider, sew with awl and sinew, and cut and make moccasins, clothing, and tent covers. There was always plenty of work to do, but I had time to rest, and go to see my friends, and I was not given tasks beyond my strength. My father did the heavy lifting. . . . He was a kind man, and helped my mothers and me when we had hard work to do. . . . For my industry in dressing skins, my clan aunt, Sage, gave me a woman's belt. . . . Only a very industrious girl was given such a belt. . . . To wear a woman's belt was an honor.

According to Waheenee, terrible changes had come to the Mandan-Hidatsa people after they were removed to new reservation lands and forced to do everything, including

continued on page 65

COMMON THREADS

As reflected in their artwork, Indian women are bound to one another by many common threads, even though they come from diverse groups, live in varied rural and urban areas, and enjoy many different levels of education—ranging from elementary to graduate school.

Much of their art expresses a concern with the history, culture, and spirituality of their people. Female Indian artists commemorate past events. They draw upon ceremonies and legends for symbolic references to traditional life and to their own inner world. And they infuse their art with a feeling for the earth—its colors, shapes, and materials. Their heritage informs their work.

Indian women also strive to transcend tradition and combat the romanticization of the past. They comment on modern Indian life, create new forms and images, borrow techniques from other cultures, and work in media that traditionally belong to Indian men or to non-Indians.

Yet even while they cross boundaries, opening new doors to their sisters and teaching others about the realities of Indian life, these artists maintain a spiritual contact with the past. For modern Indian women, the act of creating art is ritualistic, much like the traditional tasks of grinding corn or pressing and scraping animal skins. The process of making art is as important as the final product.

On the following pages are examples of the work of eight Indian women who have had pieces of art on exhibit at the American Indian Community House Gallery/Museum, the only Indian-owned gallery in New York City.

Untitled, from series Coming into Power, hand-tinted/hand-painted black-and-white photograph, by Wolf Clan Cherokee artist Shan Goshorn.

My People Are Sacred, *acrylic/oil/collage on paper, 1991, by Jane Ash Poitras, a Cree from Fort Chipewyan, Alberta, Canada. This work commemorates the Battle of Wounded Knee and the OKA incident in Canada. The shields at the bottom represent the supernatural powers that warriors took with them into battle. These powers could be transferred by the shaman to other members of the tribe, such as children. "Indians today are wounded warriors," says the artist. "They must fight to recapture their spirit and balance."*

Wounded OKA, *acrylic/oil/collage on paper, 1990, by Jane Ash Poitras. In the OKA incident, the construction of a golf course threatened sacred Mohawk land, but the Indians won their case in court.*

Resurrecting Fossil Fish, *acrylic on canvas, 1987, by Karen Coronado, a Lumbee from North Carolina. This piece represents an attempt to recapture the sensibilities of a lost heritage.*

Cedar Woman Spirit, *acrylic paint/paper, hand-made from cedar/silk background, 1988.*

Killer Whale Child, *acrylic paint/paper, handmade from cedar/silk background, 1988.*

As a small child in Petersburg, Alaska, Tlingit artist Edna Jackson learned from her mother how to make playthings out of objects collected on beaches and in the woods. Influenced by these early experiences, she makes use of natural materials, as well as paper made from bark and grasses, in her art today.

60

Red Bear Mask, *rope/wood metallic yarn/beads/ribbon/feathers/nickelsilver, 1987, by Gail Tremblay, an Onondaga. By unifying materials that have different textures, Tremblay hopes to explore that which makes "the human spirit dance."*

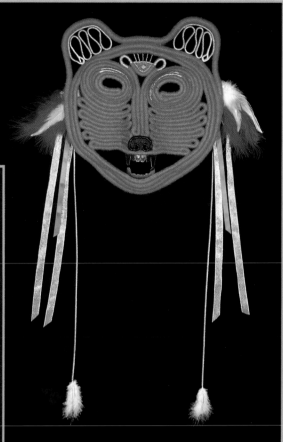

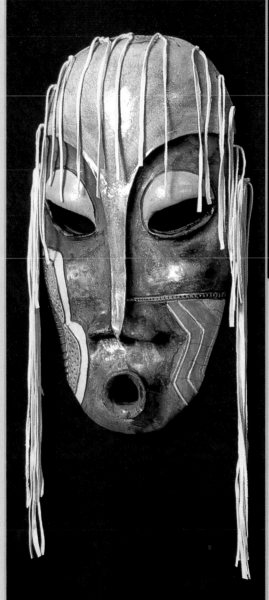

Pheasant Woman, *Raku/leather, 1988, by Lillian Pitt, a Yakima from Warm Springs, Oregon. After firing her masks using Raku—a reduction process developed in 16th-century Japan—Pitt smolders them in beds of corn husks or grass and dresses them with feathers or buckskin fringe. Her work, she says, allows her to express how she feels about the earth.*

The imagery in her art, Linda Lomahaftewa says, "comes from being Hopi and remembering shapes and colors from ceremonies and the landscape. I associate a special power and respect, a sacredness, with these colors and shapes, and this carries over into my own work."

Fragments of a Rainbow, *acrylic and rice paper on linen, 1988.*

Blue Cloud Maiden, *mono-type with oil pastel, 1989.*

In this monoprint, entitled The Female City Sky, *by Santa Clara Pueblo/Navajo artist Beverly R. Singer, a buffalo leaps across sky-scrapers and a muddy river, demonstrating the persevering spirit of Indian women in urban settings. Like the buffalo, says Singer, women are a reservoir of freedom and strength. In the Pueblo tradition, Buffalo women dance every winter and spring to restore life-giving energy to their tribe.*

Because Indian art is often thought of as having no ties to present life or to non-Indians, photography is critical to Shan Goshorn's work. "I want the viewer to realize that my subjects are . . . part of today. We are a contemporary people with strong roots in a traditional world."

Harmony for Our Seventh Generation, *hand-tinted black-and-white photocollage.*

Weaving in the Night, *hand-tinted/hand-painted black-and-white photograph.*

Members of the Blood women's Matoki Society, the Motokiks, put up their meeting lodge in the center of a Sun Dance camp in 1891. After the government banned the performance of ceremonies, songs, and dances, women who had once been central to their tribe's rituals experienced a decrease in social status.

continued from page 56

farming, the way that whites did. Regardless of the altered Hidatsa way of life, however, Waheenee held to traditional culture. She stated, "I cannot forget our old ways. Often in summer I rise at daybreak and steal out to the cornfields, and as I hoe the corn I sing to it, as we did when I was young. No one cares for our corn songs now."

It would be nearly one hundred years—not until after World War II—before some restoration of old behaviors and systems of achievement and honor returned to Indian peoples. In the wild West shows and in military service, a few men could regain some of the status and dignity that they once had as leaders and warriors. For women, the path was more difficult.

Other changes forced upon Indian culture during the late 19th century came about because of Christian influence. Missionaries urged the Indians to abandon "savage" practices, such as polygamy. Traditionally, a woman may have lived with her sisters, sharing a husband as well as the work. Because Christians insisted that men live with

In this photo by Gilbert Wilson, Buffalo Bird Woman, or Waheenee (left), slices peeled prairie turnips, using an old buffalo-horn spoon as a cutting block. Although removal to reservation lands facilitated the deterioration of traditional Hidatsa culture, Waheenee held to many of the old ways.

only one wife, families were split up, and people were forced to work far away from their relations.

Assimilation into white culture also affected the nature of relationships within a family. In a most revealing passage in her 1883 autobiography *Life Among the Piutes*, Sarah Winnemucca Hopkins describes the traditional relationship of a Northern Paiute husband and wife during the time of childbirth:

> Both mother and father fast from all flesh, and the father goes through the labor of oiling the wood for twenty-five days, and assumes all his wife's household work during that time. If he does not do his part in the care of the child, he is considered an outcast. . . . The young mothers often get together and exchange their experiences about the attentions of their husbands; and inquire of each other if the fathers did their duty to their children and were careful of their wives' health.

All that, she explains, changed because white men tried to teach Indian men to scorn the ways of the past, when they cared for children and for their wives.

Also, as part of the government's assimilation efforts, children were taken away to school to receive a non-Indian education. This experience was often extremely traumatic for Indian children, who were accustomed to living very close to all their family. In 1906, in her autobiography *Me and Mine*, Helen Sekaquaptewa, a Hopi woman, told of being taken away by force to school.

> We were now loaded into wagons hired from and driven by our enemies. . . . We were taken to the schoolhouse . . . into the big dormitory, lighted with electricity. . . . I had never seen so much light at night. . . . Evenings we would gather . . . and cry softly so the matron would not hear and scold or spank us. . . . I can still hear the plaintive little voices saying, "I want to go home. I want my mother." We didn't understand a word of English and didn't know what to say or do.

Some children died far away in boarding schools, such as the Hampton Institute in Virginia. Some girls married white men and never came home. Those who returned to their people no longer displayed Indian cultural behavior or spoke their native language. Many whose parents had died were sent to orphanages to work in the houses of missionaries or wealthy people in cities. These experiences forced young Indian men and women to accept the circumstances of change and live in their altered world. Many schools were established for this very purpose—to assimilate Indian children into the white world.

The Cherokee Female Seminary was established in 1850 by Cherokee chief John Ross, the Cherokee Council, and missionaries to the Cherokee Nation. Although the Seminary represented some extraordinary means used by the Cherokee people to assure their own survival, it also represented accessions to a white life.

Modeled after Mount Holyoke Seminary (later Mount Holyoke College), which had educated a number of Cherokee women, the Cherokee Female Seminary was established at Park Hill Mission, a few miles from Tahlequah, Oklahoma, the Cherokee capital. When the seminary burned down in 1887, tribe members and citizens of Tahlequah rebuilt the school in the town. In 1909, it was renamed the Northeastern State Normal School, which became Northeastern Oklahoma State University when the campus and buildings were purchased by the state.

The Cherokee, long advocates of universal education for men and women—a feature of life not at all

Female students at an Indian School in Santa Fe, New Mexico (ca. 1904). In this government school, which was designed to assimilate Indian children into the white world, the girls were far more confined than the boys.

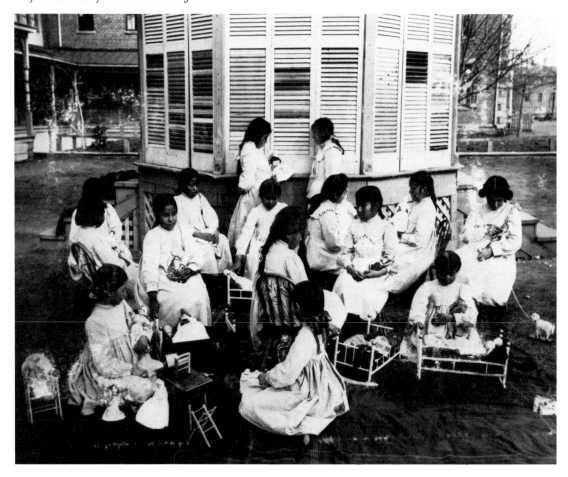

In the late 19th century, the Cherokee Female Seminary employed non-Indians to teach Latin, English, and other courses that were thought to help young Indian women endure the white world. Some assimilated entirely. Others used their knowledge of white ways to lead their people to resist extinction.

guaranteed to women in white society—built the seminary to reinforce traditional Cherokee education, which they had been forced to abandon during removal. But these new institutions, unlike their school in the Southeastern Cherokee homelands, did not appear to achieve this objective.

The new schools were profoundly Christian and European in their orientation. Latin, English, and other non-Indian subjects constituted the course of study, and the seminary was taught primarily by non-Indian women from schools in the East. The school even favored those students who were mixed-blooded daughters of well-to-do farmers and kept mixed-blooded girls apart from full-blooded girls. The teachers and administrators, who were also non-Indian, worked to obliterate Indian values from a child's education. In effect, the seminary trained hundreds of young women in the skills they would need to endure the white world.

Ironically, however, many Indian women used the education and "civilization" afforded them by forced schooling and Christianization to lead their people to resist extinction. Armed with knowledge of white manners and values, these women were central to the reform and resistance movements through which many tribal peoples, though virtual captives of the United States, would resist non-Indian efforts to destroy their culture. Indeed, as one Blackfeet saying goes, "a nation is not conquered until the hearts of its women are on the ground." ▲

Sarah Winnemucca, shown here in her "Princess" outfit, spoke to American audiences across the nation to call attention to the problems of her people, the Paiute.

EARLY MODELS
OF
REFORM

Beginning in the late 19th century, a number of Indian women found ways of resisting those government policies and non-Indian practices that worked to obliterate native cultures. One such individual was Sarah Winnemucca, who was born into the rapidly changing world of the Paiute. She saw her people, who had once controlled a vast hunting-and-living range in present-day Nevada, become increasingly impoverished and desperate after the tribe was confined to a reservation in Reno in 1860.

During these hard times, settlers, soldiers, and Indian agents clashed repeatedly with the Paiute over rights to the land. In 1879, the Paiute were again moved, and for a while they lived peacefully in their new home in Oregon. But in 1878 war broke out among the Bannock people, the Paiute's old enemy. Winnemucca, who had been trained at mission schools, volunteered as a U.S. Army scout and interpreter, believing that the army might protect the Paiute against the Bannock and the depredating whites, who constantly thirsted for more territory to conquer.

When the Paiute were removed again in a brutal starvation winter trip and confined with the Bannock to the Yakima Reservation in Washington, Sarah secured a presidential order for their return to Oregon. However, the agents at the reservation and the army would not let them relocate. Sarah then went on the lecture circuit, in her fanciful "Princess" outfit, becoming a mesmerizing advocate for her people's rights. She describes in her autobiography their struggles and her efforts to restore them to their dignity. Of women's participation in matters of decision making among her people, she wrote:

> The women know as much as the men do, and their advice is often asked. . . . The council-tent is our Congress, and anybody can speak who has anything to say, women and all. They are always interested in what their husbands are doing and thinking about. And they take some part even in the wars. They are always near at hand when fighting is going on, ready to snatch up their husbands and carry them off if wounded or killed. . . . If women could go into your Congress, I think justice would soon be done to the Indians.

In spite of her success in calling the American public's attention to the Paiute's problems, however, the government refused to act on their behalf. Winnemucca died in 1891 without seeing the restoration of the Paiute's rights.

Many other Indians concerned with bettering the conditions of their people were equally frustrated by the government's intransigence but tried to effect change through reform, by appealing to non-Indians for new legislative action. Various members of one Omaha Indian family, the LaFlesches, fought for their people through the non-Indians' system of governance and education.

The father, Joseph LaFlesche, or Iron Eyes, was an Omaha chief deter-

mined to see his people survive the reservations. His son, Francis, one of the first Indian anthropologists, was himself committed to preserving and protecting traditional Indian culture from the encroachments of white society's civilization policies. Joseph LaFlesche's brother, the Ponca leader Standing Bear, brought one of the most important cases for Indian rights to court, sacrificing his health and political standing in the process. Joseph LaFlesche's two daughters, Suzette and Susan, lobbied Congress and the public to honor treaties and to deal with Indians respectfully.

Susan LaFlesche, who had trained at the Hampton Institute and the Women's Medical College in Philadelphia, was the first female Indian physician. Her medical education, supplemented by visits to museums, musical performances, and the sights of the urban East, was financed by a reform group known as the Women's National Indian Association. As a medical missionary to the Omaha, she treated cholera, dysentery, influenza, and many other diseases that were rampant among the population. She also spent much of her lifetime trying to call attention to the alcoholism and disease that destroyed many of her people. She attributed much of the problem to the slaughter of the Plains buffalo and the subsequent failure of the Omaha's economy.

Appearing in both dress and speech to be a well-educated, upper-middle-class woman, Susan LaFlesche went on the lecture circuit, often with her sister,

Susan LaFlesche (center) on the day of her graduation from the Hampton Institute in 1886. To her left are George Bushotter (Sioux, Lower Brule) and Anna Dawson (Arikara); to her right are Rebecca Mazakute (Sioux, Crow Creek) and Charles Picotte (Sioux, Yankton). LaFlesche later became the first female Indian physician and for much of her life lobbied for her people's rights.

Suzette, to tell people the truth about the Indians' condition. She lobbied for the eradication of tuberculosis and disease spread by flies. She also campaigned for individual ownership of land on reservations and fought against extending the trust periods so that the Omaha and others could lease, sell, and use their lands without government intervention.

Plagued by increasing ill health, she continued to fight against the incompetence and corruption of the government as well as against those laws that contributed to the dependency and demoralization of Indian people. She insisted that the Omaha were "independent and self-reliant . . . as competent as the same number of white people." Realizing that liquor was used

Suzette LaFlesche sat for this photo in non-Indian clothing. However, recognizing that traditional garments appealed to whites, she wore Omaha ceremonial clothing when standing before audiences in America and Europe, lecturing on the theft of Indian lands and the corruption of government agents.

as a means of getting Indians to sign over lands and goods, she became more and more of a prohibitionist and lobbied to ban alcohol on reservations.

Suzette, born in 1854, was trained in reservation mission schools and in private schools in the East and was fluent in French. Known on the lecture circuit as Bright Eyes (the English translation of her Omaha name, Insta Theumba), Suzette was assisted in publicizing her people's situation by her husband, journalist Thomas Tibbles. She often traveled with Tibbles and with her uncle Standing Bear. Not unlike the "Princess" Sarah Winnemucca, Suzette dressed in her Omaha ceremonial clothing and lectured in America and Europe on the disappearance of the buffalo, the breaking of treaties, the theft of Indian lands under the General Allotment Act, and the corruption among government agents.

From her own family experience, she learned that Indians were not "persons" in the U.S. legal system, that no Indian could expect protection under the law in court. Outraged by government policies that increasingly forced Indians to depend on the government for essentially every need, she was most intent upon their becoming citizens and enjoying full protection under the Constitution. Before she died in 1903 at the age of 49, she wrote to a friend:

> It is more than ten years since we went to our last hunt. The poles of the holy tent [for the Sun Dance] remain. We camp no more in the great circle. The young are passing into another life. I have thought much of my father during this visit. His wish was for his children to walk in the Good Road. I hope we have found the Good Road of which he dreamed.

Although Sarah Winnemucca and the LaFlesche sisters, through their political activism, strived to draw the attention of non-Indians to the problems suffered by Indian peoples, not all reformers were as overtly political in their approach to reform. Emily Pauline Johnson, born to an Englishwoman and a Mohawk chief in Canada, was the granddaughter of the council speaker for the Iroquois Confederacy. Both her father and grandfather were noted orators, and Johnson loved reading and theatrical performance.

In addition to writing poetry and acting on the stage, Johnson became a political activist. She had seen her father battle against the white liquor and timber traffic on the reserve. He had been beaten severely by whites several times for his efforts, beatings that finally killed him.

Johnson began her life as a writer and actress in Toronto in 1892. Her first readings were taken from poems about Louis Riel's mixed-blood war of resistance against the Canadian government in 1870. She soon took the name of her great grandfather, Tekahionwake, and published several volumes of poetry and collections of stories and articles. She traveled in Canada, the United States, and Europe, performing her stories and reading from her poetry.

Johnson was very concerned with the image of Indian women. She once said, "I am a Redskin, but I am something else too—I am a woman." She filled her stories with Indian heroines and wrote extensively of marriage between the races—a theme that obsessed missionaries, who frequently wrote and preached to whites against such marriages. Principally, however, her stories concerned the inevitable conflict between Indians and whites and spoke of the necessity for respect between the cultures.

Although she performed in buckskin dresses, a costume not at all characteristic of her people's dress, and her poetry was very much of the romanticist type common to the times, Johnson's work was often directed at righting the wrongs and injustices Indians had withstood from the white world. She created romanticized stereotypes and idealized heroines in order to repudiate the image of the bloodthirsty savage so common in Canada and the western United States. As a writer, artist, and activist, Johnson set a tone so often followed by other Indian writers, particularly female, in the 19th and 20th centuries.

In American Indian societies on the whole, women may have had many rights withheld from them by the mainstream society, but they also perceived that even white females in America had been denied their rights. Thus, Indian women lobbied for reforms that benefited not only Indians but all races of women as well. It is no wonder that Indians became, in many ways, a central symbol for some reforms.

Suffragists such as Matilda Gage, Elizabeth Cady Stanton, Susan B. Anthony, and Alice Fletcher (another ethnologist who gained much of her

Emily Pauline Johnson directed her works at righting the wrongs and injustices Indians had withstood from the white world. As a writer, artist, and activist, she set a tone adopted by many other Indian women in the 19th and 20th centuries.

knowledge from the LaFlesche family) noted how the life enjoyed by Indian women differed from that of European and American women. Iroquois society in the state of New York offered these reformers a chance to observe the life of Iroquois women. Many observations made about Iroquois society were later confirmed by Fletcher to be true of other Indian cultures as well.

Although non-Indian reformers may not have entirely understood how an Indian woman's power and authority were exercised in everyday life, they did recognize that the principles upon which most Indian societies were organized conferred upon Indian women a status very different from that of their white counterparts. In 1888, Fletcher spoke before the International Council of Women, noting that an Indian wife never submits entirely to her husband:

> Her kindred have a prior right and can use that right to separate her from him or protect her from him, should he mistreat her . . . not only does the woman (under our white nation) lose her independent hold on her property and herself, but there are offenses and injuries which . . . would be avenged and punished by relatives under tribal law, but which have no penalty or recognition under our laws. . . . At the present time, all property is personal . . . a wife is as independent in the uses of her possessions as is the most independent man in our midst. . . . When I was living with the Indians, my hostess one day gave away a very

fine horse. . . . I asked, will your husband like to have you give the horse away? . . . I tried to explain how a white woman would act, but laughter and contempt met my explanation of the white man's hold upon his wife's property . . . . As I have tried to explain our statutes to Indian women, I have met with one response. They have said, "As an Indian woman, I was free. I owned my home, my person, the work of my hands, and my children could never forget me. I was better as an Indian woman than under white law."

Later, Nancy Lurie, an anthropologist and adopted Winnebago, would write:

> Whether the cosseted darling of the upper class or the toil-worn pioneer farm wife, the white woman was pitifully dependent through life on the whims and fortunes of one male, first a father and then a husband. Bereft of virtually any political rights, she also lacked the security of a tribe who would then be committed to care for her if she were orphaned or widowed. Traditionally the poor white woman was left with the denigrating embarrassment of accepting charity.

These perceptions prompted early-20th-century feminists to look partly to Indian models for the rhetoric of reform and, moreover, to seek out the speeches and instructions of such female Indian reformers as the LaFlesches.

Representatives of the National Council of American Indians, headed by founder and president Gertrude Simmons Bonnin (third woman from right), visit the studio of Ulric Dunbar, a noted sculptor. The statue of Sitting Bull in the center was later placed in the Wyoming Historical and Archaeological Museum in Wilkes-Barre, Pennsylvania.

Perhaps no one better exemplifies the role and activism of modern Indian women than Gertrude Simmons Bonnin, also known as Zitkala-sa, a Sioux woman who participated in and helped organize the modern Indian reform and pan-Indian movement. In the early 20th century, a group of Indian activists, including two physicians, Dr. Carlos Montezuma and Charles Eastman, organized the Society of American Indians (SAI). These well-educated people gathered to lobby for Indian self-determination, though within the boundaries of models developed from the majority society.

Although the SAI was male dominated, a number of women contributed organizational skills and participated in the group's political activities. Like their male counterparts, most of the women were very well educated and assimilated into white society. Nora McFarland, from the Carlisle Indian school, Rosa LaFlesche, of the Omaha Indian family, Alice DeNomie, a Chippewa, and Marie Baldwin, an attorney and suffragette, were among the many women who helped run the organization in Washington and elsewhere. Eventually, some women served as officers on the SAI's council, but Gertrude Bonnin became the first to appear on the society's board of editors.

Bonnin, a classically trained violinist, wrote articles and stories that appeared in major magazines. She rebelled against the traditional role assigned to her by both Sioux and white society, and her political activism allowed her to escape some of the restrictions imposed on her by both worlds. On the Uintah Reservation in Utah, where her Sioux husband (Raymond Bonnin) held a federal job, she developed cooking, sewing, and hygiene classes for the "social betterment" of reservation residents and began taking an active role in the SAI's business.

Eventually, after moving to Washington, D.C., Bonnin stopped writing articles on domestic life and turned to such issues as land and water rights. When the SAI began to fail in 1926, she formed the National Council of American Indians, a major Indian lobbying group. She became the organization's president; her husband, its secretary. In response to criticism of her ambitions from Indian men, Bonnin also began to

Hopi artist Nampeyo (1860–1942), shown here in a photograph taken in 1885, invented many new designs in pottery ware and reconstructed old designs and forms that had not been produced among her people for many centuries.

write on the historical role of women leaders. She and other women, such as Alice Lee Jemison, a Seneca and another controversial native naturalist, would set the stage for an ever-increasing presence of Indian women in the national and pantribal political movements of the 1960s.

During the period of reform in the early 20th century, native peoples also experienced a cultural revival. With the increased ease of travel after the completion of transcontinental railway lines in the late 19th century and with the economic boom in the United States following World War I, the West was once again overrun by whites. Some, like those before them, sought the fortunes that had eluded them in the East; others were looking for exotic landscapes and cultures that they could no longer find in the increasingly crowded, urbanized, industrialized landscape of the East.

The enormous pressures on tribal cultures caused by tourism and economic adventurism in the West and Southwest undoubtedly created many changes in Indian life. In the midst of poverty as a result of the loss of access to traditional land and water resources, many native women used traditional skills to create art objects that were marketable. In the Southwest, Northwest, Northeast, and Great Lakes, tourists bought baskets, pottery, and many other beautiful material goods. In effect, female Indian artisans revived the older and dormant women's societies for the purposes of survival.

Nampeyo (1860–1942), a Hopi artist, created what historians would later call the Sikyatki Revival of Hopi pottery. Inspired by the excavated pottery found first accidentally by Hopi and later by archaeologists in the 1890s, Nampeyo began to reconstruct old designs and forms that had not been produced among the Hopi for many centuries. Her work was discovered and promoted by railroad hotels and tourist shops, whose appearance had just begun to transform the Southwest into a tourist paradise.

In truth, Nampeyo did not simply copy old designs but invented designs and forms based on the old ware, thus revising—while preserving—the symbols essential to her people's cultural heritage. The work of Nampeyo and another woman, a Pueblo from San Ildefonso named Maria Martinez, attracted attention to Pueblo pottery and inspired many other Indian artists to revitalize and invigorate traditional forms.

A Cheyenne woman, Mary Little Bear Inkanish, and other Cheyenne and Kiowa women in southern Oklahoma formed a new women's society in the 1930s. Frustrated in their ability to earn money during the Great Depression, a group of women formed the Woman's Heart Society to make goods decorated with beadwork, moccasins, and other items to sell. Although they remembered that their mothers and grandmothers had belonged to secret societies of the best craftswomen, none of the women had ever been a member of

Pueblo Indian Maria Martinez, shown here (ca. 1937) with her husband, Julian, inspired many other Indian artists to revitalize and invigorate traditional art forms.

THE PARTS OF A POET
Wendy Rose (Hopi/Miwok)

Loving

the pottery goodness
of my body

       settled down on flowers
       pulling pollen in great
       handfuls; full & ready

       parts of me are pinned
       to earth, parts of me
       undermine song, parts
       of me spread on the water,
       parts of me form a rainbow
       bridge, parts of me follow
       the sandfish, parts of me
       are a woman who judges.

one because most societies disappeared after Indians were placed on reservations.

The women who formed the Woman's Heart Society adopted each other into their tribe. Eventually, they took their beadwork far away to the Gallup New Mexico Intertribal Ceremony and opened up the modern crafts market for other beadworkers from Oklahoma and the Southern Plains. As a result of these efforts, Mary Little Bear Inkanish was asked to teach crafts through the newly formed Indian Arts and Crafts Board, and many more women learned arts that might have been lost forever.

Indian women were also in the forefront of efforts to preserve Indian languages and oral traditions. Among them were Sioux linguist and folklorist Ella Deloria and the Okanogan novelist and folklorist Humishuma (also known as Christal Quintasket). They and others labored to save Indian languages and create an entirely new collected body of traditional song, narrative, and drama as well as new literature using non-Indian models. Many had been informants for anthropologists, who interviewed them to find out what the past was like. They then chose to become scholars in their own right, acting to preserve the traditions that many believed were dead or dying. Like the Clackamas storyteller Victoria Howard, they set down the body of folkloric materials that male scholars claimed for themselves and on which the present-day understanding of native literatures is built. They would also set an example for others later in the 20th century, commanding participation of Indian women as scholars and writers.

In spite of the Indian woman's political activism and efforts to revive her culture in the late 19th and early 20th centuries, she could not vote in federal elections unless she renounced tribal citizenship, served in the military, and took an oath of citizenship. Non-Indian women secured the vote in 1919, but not until 1924 were all Indian women and men granted that right.

Frank Matsura photographed these two Indian women, dressed in Victorian clothing, outside of Colville Indian Reservation in Washington (ca. 1910). At the time, although many Indians worked outside the reservation in white establishments, they did not enjoy the rights and benefits of U.S. citizenship.

Having citizenship and the vote, however, could do little to change the Indians' conditions until the federal government changed its Indian policies. In the 1930s, some of the reforms that had thus far eluded native peoples became possible. A new commissioner of the Bureau of Indian Affairs, the anthropologist John Collier, saw reform as essential. He and other like-minded officials halted the government's policies of assimilation, Christianization, and civilization, thus stopping at least the official assaults on Indian life, language, and culture. Although life on the reservations did not completely change for the better, Collier initiated certain reforms in tribal governance that brought a new atmosphere to federal Indian policy. Indians were at last allowed some power to determine their own course. ▲

In 1988, attorney Sue Williams (Sioux) became the first Indian woman to argue a case before the Supreme Court. Indian women in both the United States and Canada have equipped themselves with the tools necessary to affect federal reform and have fought to preserve native traditions.

AT THE HELM
OF
THE FUTURE

Women across the United States experienced dramatic changes in their life because of the demands of World War II. Many were recruited from rural areas to fill industrial and war-related jobs in the cities. Airplane factories, asbestos plants, army ordnance depots, shipyards, and other industries employed a substantial percentage of Indian women, most of whom had never before been off the reservation.

Whether white, black, or Indian, most women were forced to relinquish their jobs to returning veterans, or they simply lost the position because production decreased at the end of the war. A number of Indian women as well as Indian men had voluntarily joined the armed forces. When the Servicemen's Readjustment Act, or G.I. Bill of Rights, was passed in 1944, some veterans took the opportunity to obtain a higher education; others had gained skills during the war that helped them land jobs. Afterward, many Indian women went to work in Indian schools, serving as dormitory matrons, cooks, or on the janitorial staff; some found work in urban areas as domestics and waitresses.

In spite of the many economic and social reforms instituted by President Franklin Roosevelt during the depression era of the 1930s and the postwar era of the 1940s, veterans found little work on reservations. Although the rest of rural America benefited from government projects designed to improve roads and provide communities water and electricity, reservations saw little improvement. Because industrialization and other forms of "modernization" had passed them by, veterans began looking for jobs off the reservation.

New government policies formed at the end of the war, after John Collier resigned from office, further stilted the growth of reservation life, fueling the mass exodus to cities. One such policy was termination, which was designed to remove as many reservations as possible from the list of tribes for whom the government was legally responsible through treaty. Then Congress instigated a new policy called relocation, urging Indians to move from the reservations to cities and towns. By the late 1980s, half of the total Indian population was living off the reservation.

The relocation period traditionally included vocational placement and job training, along with other subsidies for living in the city, such as health care. But relocation did not by any means solve employment and achievement problems for Indians. Indian families, statistically larger than most families of other races, were, and still are, classified below the poverty line, at twice the national rate. Scholars such as Ann Metcalf have noted that Indians who moved to cities traded rural poverty for urban poverty. In the 1970 census, for example, urban Indian males earned twice as much as those from rural areas but still a great deal less than did white males. Indian women, like all American women, earned half of what males earned. Indian women have consistently been, in the words of one native scholar, Shirley Hill Witt, "the lowest paid, lowest ranked, most unemployed segment of the national work force."

Relocation in the 1950s affected Indian women's roles within their fami-

An Indian nurse in the U.S. armed services (ca. 1944). Many Indians, both male and female, volunteered to fight in World War II and later took the opportunity afforded them by the Servicemen's Readjustment Act to obtain a higher education.

lies as well. Luise Bighorse, who moved to Flagstaff from the Navajo reservation, where women raised sheep, talked to Rayna Rapp, an anthropologist, about some of the changes:

> When I was growing up on the reservation, when I'd ask my Dad if I could go somewhere, he'd always say, "OK, but you have to ask your Mom." With money matters, even my father's paycheck, my Mother always had the last word. My mother holds the grazing permit for the entire family—aunts and uncles too—so if anyone wants to sell any livestock, they have to get her OK on it. . . . Here [off the reservation] the man and the woman are all the time discussing decisions, but here—the women don't get the last word as much.

Anthropologists such as Rapp and Metcalf, who have worked with relocated women, suggest that the autonomy and authority that women experienced when they worked out of their home were deeply undermined by life in the city, where they experienced wage labor and unemployment. They forfeited both a matrilocal way of life and their control over the means of economic production and distribution when they moved from reservations, where native traditions were more likely to be observed. However, in 1970, there were 10 percent as many Indian female-headed households as there were non-Indian female-run households.

Because urban life created great pressures on women to deny their Indian identity, many became alienated from tradition and were rejected by Indians who remained on the reservations. Those women who did maintain a network of kin-based relationships in the urban areas were often more successful in adjusting to a new way of life. Moreover, access to education and jobs meant that they developed skills and independence that might have eluded them in reservation economies and social structures.

Still, the era of the 1950s, with its termination and relocation policies, presented Indians with new battles for survival. Once again Indian women met the challenge both on and off the reservations. For example, Ada Deer aided in restoring her Menominee people to federal recognition and trust status in 1975 after the period of termination. To do so, she had to make many personal sacrifices:

> As a teenager, I saw the poverty of the people—poor housing, poor education, poor health. I thought, this isn't the way it should be. . . . I wanted to help the tribe in some way. . . . People said I was too young, too naive. . . . I dropped out of law school. That was the price I had to pay to get involved. . . . I spent six months in Washington influencing legislation and mobilizing the support of our people throughout the country. . . . The land was restored to trust status. . . . Where

A Navajo woman and man slaughtering a sheep on their reservation in Arizona in 1954. To-day, Navajo women on the reservation usually have the final say in family discussions con-cerning money, grazing rights, or the sale of livestock. According to Luise Bighorse, women who moved off the reservation often experienced a decrease in their authority.

did the manpower and the womanpower come to accomplish this? It came from the people.

As with the early attempts to educate and Christianize Indian people, relocation and termination policies backfired. Those efforts, instead of creating a better atmosphere for assimilation and civilization, in many instances produced a new population of educated Indian people who turned their newfound skills into tools for political and cultural activism.

Since the 1970s, in what has generally been thought of as a period of self-determination, one very important goal of Indian peoples has been the reclamation of their cultural and political autonomy. In 1975, this objective was legitimized when the government approved the Indian Self-Determination Act. During the next five years, federal appropriations were directly administered to tribal governments, and Indians began to make their own decisions about how to spend the funds.

Because Indians began to agitate for their rights, other legislative acts were passed. In a 1970 interview, Ramona Bennett, a Puyallup activist, described her people's struggle to regain their fishing rights in Washington State:

At this time our people are fighting to preserve their last treaty right—the right to fish. . . . Fishing is part of our art forms and religion and diet, and the entire culture is based around

it. . . . Our people have fought a legal battle for more than forty-nine years. . . . Our source [the salmon] is being depleted. . . . Finally, we said this is enough. . . . At that time, I was a member of Puyallup Tribal Council and I was a spokesman for the camp. And I told them [the police] what our policy was: that we were there to protect our Indian fishermen.

In the last three decades, native people have carried on a debate, sometimes a violent struggle, with non-Indians over methods of hunting and fishing (e.g., spearfishing, gillnetting) allowed non-Indians; fishing and hunting quotas guaranteed by treaties and reaffirmed by the courts; water rights; religious rights; and government intervention in Indian affairs. Indian women have placed themselves in the midst of the struggles.

A number of native women's organizations sprang up in the 1970s and 1980s to address the extraordinary assaults on native culture. Throughout the United States and Canada, as well as Greenland, native women have organized themselves into groups. Among these are the White Buffalo Calf Society, the Native Women's Association of Canada, the Women of All Red Nations, the Inuit Women's Association, the Women's Dance Health Program, and the Sacred Shawl Society. All have remarkably similar goals because the problems and dilemmas their people face are common to all natives.

In one of many native protests in the late 1960s and early 1970s, Indian women and men occupied Alcatraz Island in San Francisco Bay for 19 months, calling for the government to build an Indian cultural center there. This woman has set her canvas tipi on a summit overlooking the Golden Gate Bridge.

Principally, these women's groups are concerned with the continuity and health of all their people. Their objectives include preventing family violence and alcohol and drug abuse; training midwives; improving educational systems and opportunities for education; supporting cultural preservation, especially that of tribal languages; and preventing the loss of a subsistent way of life.

Indian women have also come together to tackle specific issues concerning government regulation of Indian affairs. For example, native women in Canada have been especially active in lobbying for government reform of laws that deprive Indian women of federal status. (An Indian without status is one that is not recognized as an Indian by the Canadian government.)

In accordance with a body of laws and regulations called the Indian Acts, Indian women who marry a non-Indian or non-status Indian automatically lose membership in their tribe—in effect, losing status. Indian men, however, would not lose status by marrying non-status Indians or non-Indians.

In order to change the Canadian Indian Acts from their discriminating position against them, Indian women began to organize. And when the chiefs and band councils would not listen to them, they began to struggle on their own, without the help of the men. Nora Bothwell, a Mississauga Indian woman from Ontario who had lost her status, joined with other Canadian women and lobbied to amend the Indian Acts. Although the laws changed in 1985, federal legislation continued to plague Indian women and their families. Bothwell, who was reinstated and became a

Advisory board members of Ohoyo, an American Indian women's advocacy organization founded in 1983. Seated left to right are Ruth Arrington (Creek), Delores Two Hatchet (Comanche), Joy Hanley (Navajo), and Shirley Hill Witt (Mohawk). Standing left to right are Ethel Krepps (Kiowa), Rayna Green (Cherokee), Owanah Anderson (Choctaw), Jackie Delahunt (Sioux), Ada Deer (Menominee), Marjorie Bear Don't Walk (Salish-Chippewa), and Betty Crouse (Seneca).

MADONNA OF THE HILLS
Paula Gunn Allen (Laguna/Sioux/Lebanese)

She kept finding arrowheads
when she walked to Flower Mountain
and shards of ancient pottery
drawn with brown and black designs—
cloud ladders, lightning stairs and rainbirds.

One day
she took a shovel when she walked that way
and unburied fist-axes, manos, scrapers,
stone knives and some human bones,
which she kept in her collection
on display in her garden

She said that it gave her
a sense of peace to dig and remember
the women who had cooked and scrubbed
and yelled at their husbands
just like her. She liked, she said,
to go the spot where she'd found
those things and remember the women
buried there.

It was restful, she said,
and she needed rest . . .
from her husband's quiet alcohol
and her son who walked around dead.

---

chief in 1987, describes the effects of the Indian Acts on the survival of the community:

> Communities are supposed to be able to establish their own membership codes under Bill C-31 [the New Indian Acts] but we have already been notified that the federal government will pay for local services only for those members who qualify under the Indian Acts. If we at Alderville have all our people back without restrictions, we will always have a community. If we abide by Indian Act regulations, some families, including my own, will disappear from the community in two generations.

The struggle for their rights continues, but Indian women in both the United States and Canada have equipped themselves with the tools necessary to affect federal reform. They not only lobby but also fight through the judicial system as lawyers. Native female attorneys, working directly for tribes or for law firms hired by tribes, have won landmark cases in national, state, and local courts. The victories have helped preserve native traditions.

During the last four centuries, Indian cultures have lost many traditional songs, dances, religious forms, social structures, languages, and ways of life. However, an incredibly vital traditional life has persisted among various native peoples, and women have been at the center. In the United States, Canada, and Greenland, Indian people still hunt, fish, and trap, not only for food, furs, and hides for their own use but also for cash. As has always been the case, a woman's responsibilities are enormous. As Karen Olsen, an Inuit scholar, has suggested, in addition to preparing foodstuffs and hides for use, a woman must teach these skills to her children. As in the past, she teaches them "respect for the animals. . . . She shows them what parts of the animal the hunter has to return to the earth when it is killed. . . . The children are taught the ritual ceremonials of thanking and showing respect to the land and the Animals."

Female Indian youth in fact precipitated cultural preservation, having become increasingly interested in revitalizing the languages, arts, and religious practices of their people. For instruction they looked to older relatives and tribe members. Inevitably, much of what they wanted to learn was known by women. In effect, women have been, and remain, the keepers of their culture, preserving traditions and handing them down to their children. According to native women who edited a special edition of a Canadian women's journal in the late 1980s:

> It was our grandmothers who held on to what they could of our identity as a People. . . . Oftentimes the fire would grow dim, but still our grandmothers persisted. We were taught that the time we are in is only borrowed from future generations. . . . Our thoughts, words and actions impact seven generations from now. It is these children held sacred by our Mother Earth for whom we must leave as true fire.

Agnes Vanderburg, a Salish elder and teacher, founded cultural camps to teach old skills such as tanning hides. Here, she is roasting camas root, potatolike bulbs of flowering plants that are indigenous to the western United States.

Because women such as Ella Deloria and Humishuma have searched for new ways of preserving and revitalizing their culture, there are now schools, national movements, and publications to shore up threatened Indian languages and other cultural forms. Salish elders such as Agnes Vanderburg, who is now deceased, started cultural camps to teach old skills such as hide tanning to anyone who wanted to learn.

Some women are writing about their culture, but they have found that their own people are reluctant to recall the old way of life. Beverly Hungry Wolf describes the reticence she came up against during her search for knowledge of traditional life:

> I recall that when I first started asking my grandmothers about their old ways they sometimes discouraged me and made me feel silly for having such interests. . . . Even though their belief in these traditions was very strong, they had been made to feel that there was no future in this world for their children and grandchildren if they didn't put these old ways aside.

Other native women experienced much the same and are now, like Beverly, writing down and passing on what they know to others who come after them.

Ruth Roessel, a Navajo educator, has written a book on Navajo women for her daughters and other native women. She notes, for example, that today—as in the past—some of the most respected medicine people are Navajo women in the Southwest. Changing Woman, the mother of the People in the Navajo creation story, bestowed on the Navajo many ceremonies and stories for healing and was herself a medicine woman; thus, it would not be illogical that Navajo women become healers in their society. Usually, a girl begins to learn medicine from her grandmother at an early age.

Women may hold medicine bundles, or *jish*, for healing. They may be herbalists, knowing which plants to use and prescribe; helpers or apprentices; or diagnosticians, responsible for determining what is wrong with a patient and what ceremony and procedure will help in curing him or her.

With the Navajo, not only do healers have an extensive knowledge of plants—a skill learned by female weavers, who must know the properties of plants to make dyes—but they also know the specific songs and ceremonies that will heal. All Navajo women need to know portions of some ceremonies, such as the puberty rite, for the well-being and traditional continuity of their family.

Thus, as activists, both on and off the reservation, and as lawyers, scholars, writers, legislators, teachers, physicians, and other professionals, Indian women have not only affected reform. They have also preserved cultural traditions. In so doing, they have become role models for their people, especially for young Indian women, and have also

Beverly Hungry Wolf (center) and her grandmothers pose for a photo in Browning, Montana, before attending an annual Medicine Pipe ceremony. Like many other Indian women, Hungry Wolf looked to her grandmothers and other female elders to learn the old ways.

become central figures of leadership in their increasingly independent native society.

During the 1960s, a number of political and civil rights protests were instigated throughout the United States. As a result of the women's movement, there has been considerable enfranchisement of women and a gradual increase in women's participation in public life. Indian women have been no exception. Although they did not take an active and visible part in the women's movement—feeling that it was unnecessary in many respects—they have become deeply involved in Indian politics.

In particular, the area in which women have been most active is in tribal governance and political leader-

Navajo author and educator Ruth Roessel gathers corn pollen to be used in her oldest daughter's puberty ceremony, called a kinaalda.

ship, on both the national and local level. Since the 1930s and 1940s, when they helped construct a national pan-Indian leadership, Indian women have taken the helm of national organizations and tribes to a greater extent than ever before.

In contemporary life, women's tribal political leadership remains concen-trated in the Far West and Alaska. In 1980 and 1981, 22 women headed tribal governments in California, the state with the largest total population of Indians; 25 women headed the Alaskan villages' corporations and tribes; 23 additional chairpersons served throughout the country. All in all, roughly 12 percent of the approximately 500 federally recognized tribes and Alaskan native corporations boasted female leadership.

Wilma Mankiller serves as a good example of a female tribal chairperson. A Cherokee raised by a farming family in eastern Oklahoma, Mankiller was a typical Indian child of the 1950s. When her family was relocated to California, Mankiller obtained an education superior to that available in rural Oklahoma. Like many coming of age in the early 1960s, she became involved in the Indian rights movement as a local community organizer.

After a college education and a failed marriage that left her with two children, Mankiller decided to return to Oklahoma, where she became involved in community development efforts in her own traditional rural Cherokee community. Perceiving the need for real self-help in that community, she gravitated toward tribal service, where her experience and knowledge could do the most good. She was so successful at integrating the needs of traditional rural communities, which had ordinarily refused to have anything to do with tribal government, that she was asked to run for deputy chief of the Cherokee Nation.

When the principal chief resigned to go to Washington as head of the Bureau of Indian Affairs, Mankiller served the remainder of his term and ran for principal chief herself. Her election to that office brought her national attention, for she was now the tribal leader of the largest Indian nation in the country.

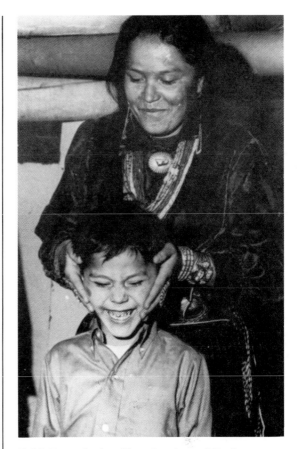

Faith Roessel, the oldest daughter of Ruth Roessel, attains the power during her kinaalda to shape the lives of others. In a symbolic act, she molds her youngest brother, Raymond.

She took advantage of the publicity to call attention to the needs and dreams of the modern Cherokee Nation.

Those who had opposed Mankiller's election had insisted that women should not serve in public office. In reply, many of her Cherokee supporters recalled the history of women's importance in public affairs. In particular,

Wilma Mankiller's leadership embodies many of the prophecies of Indian peoples from times past, which foretell that women will lead Indians into a new era. On June 15, 1991, Mankiller won her second election to the position of principal chief of the Cherokees.

they repeated Outacitty's question "Where are your women?" posed to the British delegation in the early 18th century. Outacitty, a name that is interpreted to mean Mankiller, was an ancestor of the new principal chief.

For many native people, Wilma Mankiller's leadership embodies many of the prophecies of Indian peoples from times past, which foretell a time when women will lead Indian people into a new era. Some, like the Sioux, say that the White Buffalo Calf Woman will return again to restore the buffalo.

Referring to the year 1992—a year that commemorates the first encounter between native peoples and the peoples of Europe in 1492—Mankiller discussed the return to traditional native values in *Native Peoples* magazine:

> Certainly I believe the ancient tribal cultures have important lessons to teach the rest of the world about the interconnectedness of all living things and the simple fact that our existence is dependent upon the natural world we are rapidly destroying. The traditional value systems that have sustained us throughout the past 500 years of trauma are those value systems that will bolster us and help us enter the 21st century on our own terms. Despite the last 500 years, there is much to celebrate as we approach 1992. Our languages are still strong, ceremonies that we have been conducting since the beginning of time are still being held, our governments are surviving, and most importantly, we continue to exist as a distinct cultural group in the midst of the most powerful country in the world. Yet we also must recognize that we face a daunting set of problems and issues—continual threats to tribal sovereignty, low educational attainment levels, double digit unemployment, many homes without basic amenities and racism. To grapple with these problems in a positive, forward thinking way, we are beginning to look more to our own people, communities and history for solutions. We have begun to trust our own thinking again . . . not the Columbus myth. . . . We look forward to the next 500 years as a time of renewal and revitalization for native people throughout North America.

The women of native societies have in large part been responsible for their people having something to celebrate in the modern era. They have taken on the work of reviving traditional languages and ceremonies, helping to preserve and distinguish their heritage. They have fought for their people's rights in and out of court. They have returned to their traditional native environments to lead their people through renewal. As Marlene Brant Castellano, a Canadian Huron scholar, suggests, the women continue to bend their energies to surviving:

> Native women of today are breaking their silence to lobby for improved social conditions, to protest the injustice of white man's law, to practice and teach native arts, and even to run for public office. They are

REMEMBER
Joy Harjo (Creek)

Remember the sky that you were born under,
know each of the star's stories.
Remember the moon, know who she is.
Remember the sun's birth at dawn, that is the
strongest point of time. Remember sundown
and the giving away to night.
Remember your birth, how your mother struggled
to give you form and breath. You are evidence of
her life, and her mother's, and hers.
Remember your father, his hands cradling
your mother's flesh, and maybe her heart, too
and maybe not.
He is your life, also.
Remember the earth whose skin you are.
Red earth yellow earth white earth brown earth
black earth we are earth.
Remember the plants, trees, animal life who all have their
tribes, their families, their histories, too. Talk to them,
listen to them. They are alive poems.
Remember the wind. Remember her voice. She knows the
origin of this universe.
Remember that you are all people and that all people
are you.
Remember you are this universe and that this
universe is you.
Remember all is in motion, is growing, is you.
Remember language comes from this.
Remember the dance that language is, that life is.
Remember
to remember.

Diane Burns (Chemehuevi/Ojibwa), like many other Indian writers, is a poet. Although she lives in New York City, her poetry often travels back to Lac Courte Oreilles Indian Reservation in Wisconsin.

not breaking from tradition as some have suggested. . . . Contemporary Native women have simply accepted the reality that achieving these goals in modern society requires that they put aside their reticence and work out their destiny in public as well as in private endeavor.

Perhaps native communities, in once again trusting their own way of thinking, will return to traditional forms of governance and choose to face the daunting problems of the present and future under the leadership and mutual dependence of men and women. Perhaps, as well, the non-Indian world will once again recognize that the vision and strength of Indian women is essential to the American identity. ▲

BIBLIOGRAPHY

Allen, Paula Gunn. *Spider Woman's Granddaughters: Traditional Tales and Contemporary Writing by Native American Women*. Boston: Beacon Press, 1989.

Broker, Ignatia. *Night Flying Woman: An Ojibwa Narrative*. St. Paul: Minnesota Historical Society Press, 1983.

Campbell, Maria. *Halfbreed*. Lincoln: University of Nebraska Press, 1982.

Canadian Women Studies 10, nos. 2 & 3 (Summer/Fall 1989). Special issue on Native women.

Crow Dog, Mary. *Lakota Woman*. New York: Harper's, 1990.

DeLeeuw, Adele. *Maria Tallchief: American Ballerina*. New York: Dell, 1971.

Deloria, Ella C. *Waterlily*. Lincoln: University of Nebraska Press, 1988.

Erdrich, Louise. *Love Medicine*. New York: Holt, Rinehart & Winston, 1984.

Ferrio, Jeri. *Native American Doctor: The Story of Susan LaFlesche Picotte*. Minneapolis: Carolrhoda Books, 1991.

Green, Rayna. *Native American Women: A Contextual Bibliography*. Bloomington: Indiana University Press, 1984.

————. *That's What She Said: Contemporary Fiction and Poetry by Native American Women*. Bloomington: Indiana University Press, 1984.

Hale, Janet Campbell. *The Jailing of Cecelia Capture*. New York: Random House, 1985.

Hopkins, Sarah Winnemucca. *Life Among the Piutes: Their Wrongs and Claims*. 1883. Reprint. Bishop, CA: Chalfant Press, 1985.

Hungry Wolf, Beverly. *The Ways of My Grandmothers*. New York: Morrow, 1981.

Irwin, Hadley. *We Are Mesquakie, We Are One*. Old Westbury, NY: Feminist Press, 1980.

Johnson, Emily Pauline. *Flint and Feather: The Complete Poems of Pauline Johnson*. Ontario: Mills, 1972.

Lurie, Nancy. *Mountain Wolf Woman, Sister of Crashing Thunder: A Winnebago Indian*. Ann Arbor: University of Michigan Press, 1961.

Metcalf, Ann. "Reservation-Born, City-Bred: Native American Women and Children in the City." In *Sex Roles and Changing Cultures,* edited by Ann McElroy and Carolyn Matthiasson. Buffalo: State University of New York Press, 1980.

Morrison, Dorothy. *Chief Sarah: Sarah Winnemucca's Fight for Indian Rights*. Portland: Oregon Historical Society Press, 1991.

Rachlin, Marriott, and Carol Rachlin. *Dance Around the Sun: The Life of Mary Little Bear Inkanish*. New York: Macmillan, 1977.

Roessel, Ruth. *Women in Navajo Society*. Rough Rock, AZ: Navajo Resource Center, 1981.

Silko, Leslie Marmon. *Ceremony*. New York: Viking Press, 1977.

Silman, Janet. *Enough Is Enough: Aboriginal Women Speak Out*. Toronto, Ontario: The Women's Press, 1987.

Udall, Louise. *Me and Mine: The Life Story of Helen Sekaquaptewa As Told to Louise Udall*. Tucson: University of Arizona Press, 1969.

Walters, Anna Lee. *The Sun Is Not Merciful*. Ithaca, NY: Firebrand Books, 1985.

Wilson, Gilbert. *Waheenee: An Indian Girl's Story*. Lincoln: University of Nebraska Press, 1981.

GLOSSARY

allotment U.S. policy applied nationwide through the General Allotment Act of 1887, aimed at breaking up tribally held lands by assigning individual farms and ranches to Indians. Allotment was intended as much to discourage traditional communal activities as to encourage private farming and assimilate Indians into mainstream American life.

anthropology The study of the physical, social, and historical characteristics of human beings.

assimilation The complete absorption of one group into another group's cultural tradition.

civilization program U.S. policy of the 19th and early 20th centuries designed to change the Indians' way of life so that it resembled that of non-Indians. These programs usually focused on converting Indians to Christianity and encouraging them to become farmers.

clan A multigenerational group having a shared identity, organization, and property based on belief in their descent from a common ancestor. Because clan members consider themselves closely related, marriage within a clan is strictly prohibited.

culture The learned behavior of humans; nonbiological, socially taught activities; the way of life of a group of people.

Department of the Interior U.S. government office created in 1849 to oversee the internal affairs of the United States, including government land sales, land-related legal disputes, and American Indian issues.

Indian Reorganization Act The 1934 federal law that ended the policy of allotting plots of land to individuals and encouraged the development of reservation communities. Also, the act provided for the creation of autonomous tribal governments.

Indian Territory An area in the south-central United States to which the U.S. government wanted to resettle Indians from other regions, especially the eastern states. In 1907, this area and Oklahoma Territory became the state of Oklahoma.

lineage A group of individuals related through descent from a common ancestor; a descent group whose members recognize as relatives people on the mother's side only or the father's side only.

matrilineal descent Rules for determining family or clan membership by tracing kinship through female ancestors.

missionaries Advocates of a particular religion who travel to convert nonbelievers to their faith.

myth A story of an event of the distant past. Myths often explain a practice, belief, or natural phenomenon.

oral literature A body of literary works that are communicated verbally. Oral literature, which includes songs, stories, and ritual dramas, is sometimes called "verbal arts" or "folklore."

Pan-Indian movement A renewed interest in Indian identity that spread throughout North America in the early decades of the 20th century and led to common actions by many tribes.

polygamy The practice of having more than one husband or wife at the same time.

relocation A U.S. policy of the late 20th century that encouraged Indians to leave reservations and migrate to the cities in order to enter mainstream society.

removal policy A federal policy of the early 19th century that called for the sale of all Indian land in the eastern United States and the migration of Indians from these areas to lands west of the Mississippi River.

reservation, reserve A tract of land retained by Indians for their own occupation and use. *Reservation* is used to describe such lands in the United States; *reserve,* in Canada.

stereotype A mental picture held in common by a group of people, representing an oversimplified opinion or an uncritical judgment.

termination Federal policy to remove Indian tribes from government supervision and Indian lands from government control. Termination was in effect from the late 1940s through the early 1960s.

treaty A contract negotiated between representatives of the U.S. government or another national government and one or more Indian tribes. Treaties dealt with the cessation of military action, the surrender of political independence, the establishment of boundaries, the terms of land sales, and related matters.

tribe A society consisting of several or many separate communities united by kinship, culture, language, and other social institutions including clans, religious organizations, and special groups, such as women's and men's societies.

trust The relationship between the federal government and many Indian tribes, dating from the late 19th century. Government agents managed Indians' business dealings, including land transactions and rights to national resources, because the Indians were considered legally incompetent to manage their own affairs.

ACKNOWLEDGMENTS

"Womanwork," "Grandmother," and "Madonna of the Hills" by Paula Gunn Allen. Reprinted by permission of Regents of the University of California, *Shadow Country*; La Confluencia Press, *Coyote's Daylight Trip*, both by Paula Gunn Allen.

"The Blanket Around Her" from *What Moon Drove Me To This?* and "Remember" from *She Had Some Horses* by Joy Harjo. Copyright 1980 by I. Reed Books. Reprinted with permission.

"Calling Myself Home" from *Calling Myself Home* by Linda Hogan. Copyright 1978 by Greenfield Review Press. Reprinted with permission.

"Long Division: A Tribal History" and "The Parts of a Poet" from *Lost Copper* by Wendy Rose. Copyright 1980 by Malki Museum Press. Reprinted with permission of Malki Museum Press.

PICTURE CREDITS

RAYNA GREEN, a Cherokee, is currently director of the American Indian Program at the National Museum of American History, Smithsonian Institution. Holding a Ph.D. in folklore and American studies from Indiana University, she has taught at Dartmouth University, Yale University, and the University of Massachusetts and has served on the boards of the Indian Law Resource Center and the Ms. Foundation for Women. Dr. Green has written many articles on the subject of American Indians and has compiled *That's What She Said: Contemporary Fiction and Poetry by Native American Women* as well as *Native American Women: A Contextual Bibliography.*

FRANK W. PORTER III, general editor of INDIANS OF NORTH AMERICA, is director of the Chelsea House Foundation for American Indian Studies. He holds a B.A., M.A., and Ph.D. from the University of Maryland. He has done extensive research concerning the Indians of Maryland and Delaware and is the author of numerous articles on their history, archaeology, geography, and ethnography. He was formerly director of the Maryland Commission on Indian Affairs and American Indian Research and Resource Institute, Gettysburg, Pennsylvania, and he has received grants from the Delaware Humanities Forum, the Maryland Committee for the Humanities, the Ford Foundation, and the National Endowment for the Humanities, among others. Dr. Porter is the author of *The Bureau of Indian Affairs* in the Chelsea House KNOW YOUR GOVERNMENT series.